thinking the difference

thinking the difference

For A Peaceful Revolution

Luce Irigaray

Translated from the French by
Karin Montin

Routledge
New York

First published in North America 1994 by Routledge
28 West 35th Street, New York, NY 10001

First published in France 1989 by
Librairie Générale Française, Paris
as *Le Temps De La Diffèrence: Pour une révolution pacifique*

Publisher's Note
The publishers wish to record their thanks
to the French Ministry of Culture for a grant
towards the cost of translation.

Library of Congress Cataloging-in-Publication Data:

Irigaray, Luce
[Temps de la difference. English]
Thinking the difference: for a peaceful revolution/
Luce Irigaray; translated by Karin Montin.
p. 136 cm.
Includes bibliographical references.
ISBN 0-415-90814- 0 (hbk.) — ISBN 0-415-90815-9 (pbk.)
1. Feminism. 2. Sex role. 3. Women—Psychology. I. Title
HQ1154.I74315 1994 93-40519
305.4′2—dc20 CIP

'A Chance to Live' was first published as 'Une chance de vivre' in
Sexes et parentés (Paris: Éditions de Minuit, 1987).

Typeset by Blackpool Typesetting Ltd, Blackpool
Printed and bound in Great Britain by
The University Press, Cambridge

Contents

Preface to the French Edition[1]

Thinking about the difference between the sexes is taken for granted in Italy much more than in France. In Italy, it is a matter of public and political debate, in the strict sense. It is on the agenda of the so-called separatist women's movements: for them it is a matter of constructing a specific women's identity beyond the combination of the two sexes or before any returning to a combination. It is a political objective for men, too, particularly in the PCI (Partito communista italiano, or Italian Communist Party). John Paul II's apostolic letter on the dignity of women (*Mulieris dignitatem*, autumn 1988) shows that in Italy, not even he can avoid the issue of the difference between the sexes. In response to feminist theologians there and elsewhere, John Paul II sought to claim – and in my view, not without losing the full sense of the incarnation – that man and woman are but one (?) and that any form of hierarchy that might exist between them would be the result of sin. Sin must be omnipresent, then.

But for all that, you must not think that there is no dispute in Italy on this point, especially between

Catholics and Communists. While the PCI has its own unique position on political and cultural options, and while it is far from resembling other Communist parties, to the extent that it is considering changing its name to affirm its uniqueness, and while it maintains relations with the Catholics in so far as that is possible, its position on issues such as the right to abortion and legislation respecting any form of sexual violence shows that its alliances have nothing to do with allegiance, particularly where sexual difference is concerned. The question of sexual difference is there, unavoidable, liable to cause a government to fall on a point of law concerning justice in the relations between the sexes. It makes and unmakes alliances between parties and the Church. It is present in the House and in the Senate, in trade unions, at political conventions, in the universities, in the press. It is a political and cultural force that cannot be denied.

In France, on the other hand, the difference between the sexes no longer exists! Apparently we are all equal now. Apparently we all enjoy the same rights; men and women are peers.

Obviously we cannot be talking about the same difference. The reality of the hierarchy before equality and the reality of the sexual identity in which each person enjoys rights appropriate to her or his sex are not one and the same. And denying that women and men are different in the name of some hypothetical social equality is a delusion, a bias in favour of a split – an impossible split – between private life and social identity. Out of bed or away from home, we somehow mysteriously become unisexual or asexual.

But is that as true as people believe? The *Universal*

Declaration of Human Rights [La Déclaration universelle des droits de l'homme, i.e. 'Declaration of the Rights of Man'] may be a moving document, but from the very first article, I, a woman, no longer feel 'human' [feel I am a 'man']. For I am not 'born free and equal in dignity and rights' [to other 'men']. I have female identity problems that current law does not resolve. I cannot feel that this 'universal' charter includes me unles I renounce my sex and its properties, and also agree to forget all the women who do not enjoy the minimal civil liberties that I do.

Curiously, in some countries, including France, there is almost total blindness on this point. Whether through collective psychosis or cynicism, sexual difference, which constitutes the most basic human reality, is treated like an almost non-existent problem.

Reading the *Universal Declaration of Human Rights* a little further, at Article 12 I wonder how 'privacy' is defined and how national or international justice deals with the violence of a man or male lover towards a woman. Article 21 makes me laugh outright: 'Everyone has the right of equal access to public service in his country.' Then why are so few women political leaders? Because they are not interested? Perhaps because they must shoulder the burden of 'family' responsibilities. So there is no real 'equal access'.

Let us go back to Article 17: 'No one shall be arbitrarily deprived of his property.' Fine. But what is rape then? Or the use of my naked body for advertising in the Métro? Or the exploitation of women's bodies by the pornographic media? Article 7: 'All are equal before the law and are entitled without any discrimination to equal protection of the law. All are entitled to equal protection against any discrimination in violation of this Declaration and against any incitement to such discrimination.' To whom do I report the inequality between the treatment given my body and that given a man's? What 'competent national tribunals' are there that can provide me with 'an effective remedy' [Article 8] against any act of disrespect to my physical or moral person? Just what exactly is my 'recognition [. . .] as a person before the law' (Article 6)? How can it be defended against 'cruel, inhuman, or degrading treatment or punishment' (Article 5), whether corporal or spiritual? And if I do not say the same thing as 'humans' ['men'], and, as a result, am subjected to various kinds of cruel treatment in my work, where do I turn? Must I go into exile? Change nationality? Or keep silent?

Yet, under Article 27, 'Everyone has the right to the protection of the moral and material interests resulting from any scientific, literary, or artistic production of which he is the author'. Just what does 'moral' mean here? Especially when I have long known that the law guaranteeing 'equal pay for equal work' (Article 23.2) is far from being applied equally to the two sexes.

But let us return to the basics of life, if I can call them that: 'Everyone has the right to life, liberty and the security of person' (Article 3). Where? In what context? At what time of day? I have learned the hard way that the 'right to freedom of movement' (Article 13) is not mine. More than properly dressed, well wrapped up even, in the middle of winter, I was assaulted in the rue du Commerce a few steps from my house. When I am sitting quietly at home, with the window open (am I allowed?), I wonder whether the endless planes flying overhead, wherever I may be, are not infringing upon my security, my life. But let us not talk about my freedom any more . . . It is fine for the odd fantasy or celebration once in a while, for grown-ups. For the moment I am still too small. One day, perhaps. In another world, or another History?

In short, this moving *Declaration of Human Rights* means virtually nothing in terms of my everyday reality as a woman. And I am not even subjected to the sexual 'torture' (Article 5) suffered by some of my sisters, against which I take the liberty of speaking out even though I do not have the courage to speak out on my own behalf. Nevertheless, I feel that I should begin at home, and that our civilized cultures, which have exported an industrial model for better or worse, could take the trouble to develop a just and exportable legal model with respect to the difference between the sexes.

Some communities, some countries, want nothing to do with it. The statement of general and abstract rights, defined more in terms of *against* than *for*, works as a kind of reassuring drug capable of exorcising all the dangers. But would not the best means of exorcism be reality, and specifically the reality of the difference between the sexes? Provided that neither sex has authority over the other, power is restricted by the fact that it constantly passes between woman and man, between all citizens of a country, between all living beings on this earth.

We still have a long way to go. And all the egalitarian slogans keep pushing us further back. In my opinion, all these slogans simply promote a totalitarian ideology. Respect for the difference between the sexes can protect us against this ideology without repressing or crippling our human identity. The four lectures printed here raise political and cultural issues that need to be addressed in order to develop a society in which sexual identity is treated fairly and civilly. They were originally given in Italy in response to invitations from the women of the PCI or of the Italian left. I must stress, once again, however, that the PCI cannot be imagined; it must be experienced firsthand. As I have already written, there beats 'an almost indiscernible heart of our modern societies'.[2] That heart cares about the difference that must be respected between men and women without, however, forgetting the rights gained in the name of 'equality'. That is another stage of History that we must begin and finish, together, for the present and the future.

30 June 1989

Notes to the Preface to the French Edition

1 This book was first published in Italian as *Tempo della differenza. Diritti e doveri per i sessi. Per una rivoluzione pacifica*, by Editori Riuniti, July 1989.
2 *Unità*, 17 September 1988.

Introduction

Thanks to Livia Turco's[1] invitation to speak at the women's festival in Tirrenia in 1986, I was able to get to know men and women of the PCI in a different way. The intelligence and generosity of these women and men soon made me want to work with them. Moreover, the nuclear accident at Chernobyl prompted me to come out of the relative solitude in which the newness of my thinking had placed me. I wanted to make my ideas more widely known, but not just in a transitory, limited way; I wanted to do political work in a context in which a friendly welcome, tolerance, a rejection of war and of people's oppression, and intellectual rigour were to be found. In my experience, the PCI met these criteria. I therefore decided I wanted to work with the women and men of this party.

In the eyes of some feminists, this course of action is not self-evident. But I have never called myself simply a feminist, and I feel I have very little common ground today with a good many feminists (who, incidentally, do not form a homogeneous group), especially when it comes to the relationship between political theory and practice. In my view, it is not possible to give so-called feminist university courses without being concerned with women's freedom as regards the right to contraception and, if necessary, abortion. This is just one example. There are many other women's rights that must be gained or enforced with respect to identity, work, love (especially sexual), relationships to children, and culture. In fact, women's liberation extends far beyond the framework of current feminist struggles, which are too often limited to criticizing the patriarchy, creating women's space [*l'entre-femmes*], or demanding equality with men, without proposing new values that would make it possible to live sexual difference in justice, civility and spiritual fertility.

This course of action is not necessarily self-evident, either, given a certain degree of inflexibility in the PCI. But in this party, young, or youngish, people are demanding that the political dimension be addressed from a different point of view. Through its elected representatives, notably at its XVIII Congress, the PCI announced that it intends to change its platform, particularly on the issue of women's liberation and the culture of sexual difference.

These shifts in political stance and in the organization of a society require rigorous criticism of patriarchal culture, a culture in which preference is given to male lines of descent and the society of men-amongst-themselves [*la société de l'entre-hommes*], in which women are not regarded as adults, but as men's property: family property, domestic property, sexual property, cultural property. This interpretive critique of patriarchal organization is made in the first essay in this collection, 'A Chance to Live', which was written after Chernobyl in response to Livia Turco's invitation to 'think about sexual difference as a limit to the notion of the universal and the neutral in science and knowledge'.

To explore this topic, it is essential to analyse the organization of language. Language is one of the primary tools for producing meaning: it also serves to establish forms of social mediation, ranging from interpersonal relationships to the most elaborate political relations. If language does not give both sexes equivalent opportunities to speak and increase their self-esteem, it functions as a means of enabling one sex to subjugate the other. 'How Do We Become Civil Women?' highlights some of the negative effects of the current organization of our Romance languages (effects that exist in different ways in most languages) on how the female subject is constituted, whether it is a question of the possible existence of an identity for each woman, or of increasing the standing of working women through occupational titles or through the (sex-specific) gender of objects or acquired property. The conclusion of the essay is that women's rights must be redefined so that women can tailor the rights they have gained in the name of equality to their own identity as women. Redefining rights appropriate to the two sexes to replace abstract rights appropriate to non-existent neutral individuals, and enshrining these rights in the law, and in any charter constituting some sort of national or universal declaration of human rights, is the best way for women to hold on to rights already gained, have them enforced, and gain others more specifically suited to female identity: the right to physical and moral inviolability (which means a woman's own right to virginity of body and mind), the right to motherhood free of civil or religious tutelage, women's right to their own specific culture, etc.

To create a politics of sexual difference that encompasses the most private life between persons as well as the organization of society or societies as a whole, it is useful to consider cultural change on two levels. First, the level that requires both a long-term perspective and an immediate response: changing the forms of symbolic mediation. This means, for example, changing not only the rules of speech and language that give preference to the so-called neuter masculine (the human generic called 'man', the use of the masculine plural when speaking of both sexes, etc.), but also the habitual use of images that tend to portray men as respectable citizens, as civil and religious authority figures, and consider women to be sexual property at the disposal of men. Thus, in many advertisements, the man will be wearing a tie while the woman will be partially naked. Though extreme, my example occurs frequently. Changing these habits is a long process, because it means changing attitudes, changing the cultural climate, stereotypes and customs, and so on. Yet it also requires an immediate response. We can all start letting women do half the speaking, start paying attention to how images are used at home and in society at large, and we can all start respecting each other without forgetting who we are.

But once again, these changes take place over time, and it is hard to effect all of them together because great care is needed. In the meantime, the civil law must be changed to give both sexes their own identities as citizens. This is the second level of change required. 'Civil Rights and Responsibilities for the Two Sexes' deals with the changes that must be made to the right to citizenship so that women are treated as political adults protected by the law, responsible persons with regard to civil society and the women and men that constitute it. In my view, these rights must be redefined and rewritten for our Western cultures not only out of a concern for individual and collective justice, but to give ourselves a means of communicating amongst ourselves and between cultures regardless of religious choices. Redefining the right to civil identity is one of the urgent tasks of our time, not only for the sake of living women and men, but for the sake of a possible future for the national and international community. Today, rights are increasing almost exclusively in the sphere of rights to ownership of property, benefits, various types of capital, etc. These new rights are greatly concerned with having (property) but little concerned with being(s) – women and men – and little with relationships amongst individuals based on this notion of free, responsible human identity.

The last essay in this collection, 'The Forgotten Mystery of Female Ancestry', seeks to shed light, based on mythological components still at work in our culture, on the reason why our sexual development is so impoverished and so subjected to a neutral-male libido that no longer respects the individuality of erotic partners. This essay draws parallels between the sexuality described by Freud and the sexuality of mythical figures – half-cosmic, half-god – in ancient Greece, and shows how today's erotic economy is still dominated by the man's attraction to incest with the mother and its prohibition, and the need to produce children to escape from chaos and the loss of human identity arising from eros. This sexual disaster or abandonment seems to be explained by the destruction of religious practices and myths concerning woman-as-lover (Aphrodite, for example) or human and divine relations between mother and daughter (Demeter and Kōrē/Persephone,[2] for example). To achieve a human, potentially divine, sexuality we must therefore reconsider the civil identity of each sex and rethink possible myths and religions in a way that respects the difference between the sexes.

I hope that these essays will help in creating a valid politics for both sexes. I address them in particular to my friends in the PCI, women and men, in thanks for their invitation to speak freely at their festivals and working sessions. I also dedicate them to the young women and men of this party, in the hope that they will prove useful to them in developing a body of political thought, faithful to certain of their elders, and reworked with the goal of creating a livable, happy present and future for the women and men of this world.

6 June 1989

Notes to Introduction

1 Livia Turco is a member of the PCI's national executive. She is one of a group of women currently involved in implementing a policy on women's liberation and sexual difference in Italy.
2 In most versions of this myth, the daughter of the great Goddess changes her name after being abducted by Hades [Pluto], god of the Underworld: Kōrē becomes Persephone.

1

A CHANCE TO LIVE

Tirrenia, 22 July 1986
PCI women's festival

1
A Chance to Live

The nuclear accident at Chernobyl was an earth-shattering event. Whether consciously or not, most women and men experienced it as the extreme limit of world disorder. Before Chernobyl, it was possible to hope that the general chaos or entropy of our time might at least be regulated somehow in nature. This was a serious scientific hypothesis; it was an expression of women's sociopolitical influence or power; it was the most generous solution for everyone, and the more or less blind quest of millions of people clinging to the tiniest bit of green space as if it were their only chance of survival.

But at Chernobyl, nature turned out to be a vehicle of greater destruction than any war. So now the two solutions that were said to reduce disorder – *nature* and *war* – are being reassessed. If the risk of pollution has become deadly and worldwide, nature can no longer fulfil its role of regulating energy and life, either individual or collective. And war, if it can no longer be contained within the limits of a declared conflict, can no longer be used as a means to achieve a desired end.

Some women were panic-stricken at the combination of this man-made pollution and natural phenomena: hail, storms, even sun; others felt that they must not allow themselves to become afraid of nature despite all the media warnings; many realized that the cultural disorder into which we are being drawn in spite of ourselves has become intolerable.

Since May, I have met many women and men who are physically or morally ill. I do not believe that we know exactly how these problems will affect our bodies and nature as a whole, but we do know that pollution, illness, despair and panic have increased disorder even further. Relatively simple changes must therefore be made quickly in an attempt to re-establish some sort of balance in our culture. I am not thinking solely of Chernobyl. It was a foreseeable accident that could have happened either here or there. It is another in a series of symptoms of the state of our culture, symptoms that can be found in both theory and practice. I will just mention a few so as not to put too much of a damper on your holiday. We must remember that ignorance, mixed with fear, can also cast a pall. It is better to be a little bit informed and capable of making objective decisions, minimal though they may be.

What does it mean for our entire culture to be threatened with destruction? There are, of course, declared stakes connected with threats of war. According to the types of discourse whose economy is at issue here, such threats are the sole means of maintaining international equilibrium. I shall come back to this point.

Huge amounts of capital are allocated to the development of death machines in order to ensure peace, we are told. This warlike method of organizing society is not self-evident. It has its origin in patriarchy. It has a sex. But the age of technology has given weapons of war a power that exceeds the conflicts and risks taken among patriarchs. Women, children, all living things, including elemental matter, are drawn into the maelstrom. And death and destruction cannot be associated solely with war. They are part of the physical and mental aggression to which we are constantly subjected. What we need is an overall cultural transformation, not just a decision about war *per se*. Patriarchal culture is based on sacrifice, crime and war. It is a culture that makes it men's duty or right to fight in order to feed themselves, to inhabit a place, and to defend their property, and their families and country as their property. From time to time, patriarchy must make a decision concerning war, but that is far from what is required to ensure a cultural transformation. Mankind [*le peuple des hommes*] wages war everywhere all the time with a perfectly clear conscience. Mankind is traditionally carnivorous, sometimes cannibalistic. So men must kill to eat, must increase their domination of nature in order to live or to survive, must seek on the most distant stars what no longer exists here, must defend by any means the small patch of land they are exploiting here or over there. Men always go further, exploit further, seize more, without really knowing where they are going. Men seek what they think they need without considering who they are and how their identity is defined by what they do.

To overcome this ignorance, I think that mankind needs those who are persons in their own right to help them understand themselves and find their limits. Only women can play this role. Women are not genuinely responsible subjects in the patriarchal community. That is why it may be possible for them to interpret this culture in which they have less involvement and fewer interests than do men, and of which they are not themselves products to the point where they have been blinded by it. Given their relative exclusion from society, women may, from their outside perspective, reflect back a more objective image of society than can men. Moreover, in theory, women should not be in a hierarchical relationship to men. All other types of minorities potentially are. It is with a thoroughly patriarchal condescension, either unconscious or cynical, that politicians and theoreticians take an interest in them, while exploiting them, with every possible risk of the master–slave relationship being overturned. This dialectic – or absence thereof – is built into father–son relationships, and has been since the inception of patriarchy. It is doomed to failure as a means of liberation and peace because it is based on (1) *lines of descent* insufficiently counterbalanced by a horizontal relationship between the genders and (2) *exclusively male lines of descent* making any kind of dialectic between male and female ancestries and masculine and feminine genders impossible.

The possibility of sex-specific cultural and political ethics is our best chance today. The world's economic and religious equilibrium is precarious. Moreover, the development of technology is subjecting our bodies to such trials that we are threatened with physical and mental annihilation, that our living conditions leave us no time to rest or think, whatever real leisure time we may have, and that we are continually overwhelmed, forgetful, distracted. Men's science is less concerned with prevention or the present than with curing. For objective reasons of accumulation of property, for reasons of the subjective economy of the male subject, it allows disorder and pollution to grow, while funding various types of curative medicine. Men's science helps destroy, then attempts to fix things up. But a body that has suffered is no longer the same. It bears the traces of physical and moral trauma, despair, desire for revenge, recurrent inertia. The entire male economy demonstrates a forgetting of life, a lack of recognition of debt to the mother, of maternal ancestry, of the women who do the work of producing and maintaining life. Tremendous vital resources are wasted for the sake of money. But what good is money if it is not used for life? Despite policies that encourage the birth rate for economic reasons, or sometimes for religious ones, destroying life seems to be as compulsory as giving life.

How can this contradiction – the most fundamental in most of our societies – be resolved? Not without exploring its patriarchal origins. We live in a society of men-amongst-themselves that operates according to an exclusive respect for the ancestry of sons and fathers, and of competition between brothers. And so our societies have subsumed women's ancestry under men's. Daughters are physically and culturally separated from their mothers in order to enter male families or male institutions. The family in the strict sense of the word, school, work, business, the state, information systems and most forms of recreation are organized according to male economy and law. Sexualization, which is one of the essential characteristics of living matter, has not been cultivated in our societies for centuries, and our age of technology is attempting to eliminate it. I am not referring solely to artificial means of reproduction, but to the mechanical conditioning and environment that are ours today, and which are gradually neutralizing us as sexual, living beings. I feel that the importance attached to the problem of new reproductive technologies is a way of once again reducing women to motherhood, and the couple to nothing but the reproductive function. There are much more urgent things to be taken care of on our planet as far as technological imperialism is concerned. Women's sole function has been reproducing: family and social nurturing and mothering. Animals fulfil this role as well as humans, and sometimes with more equitable task-sharing and more aesthetic sexual parading. Yet human female identity is either unknown or no longer known. Society and culture operate according to male models – genealogical and sexual.

I am going to give several examples of this drawn from a variety of fields, both theoretical and practical. With each example, I shall make a suggestion for cultural transformation.

★

1

My first examples concern the mythological, religious and symbolic foundations of our contemporary cultural and social order.

- In all public, civil and religious arenas, it is always the *man's* father or mother that counts.
- In what are called matrilineal societies, the power at issue is often associated with *male* filiation on the

mother's side: it is the mother's brother who is responsible and valued socially, thus the *son*, not the daughter, and this son ruptures the cultural relationship between mother and daughter.

- According to anthropologists, the taboo on mother–son or sister–brother incest is the basis of our sociocultural order.
- Father–son and mother–son relationships dominate our religious models. While the father–son relationship is supposed to be closer to perfection, to Christians the mother–son couple is the couple that incarnates God; it is represented at almost all religious sites, and mentioned in all Christian services.
- According to Freud, the mother–son relationship is the perfect model of desire, and love between a woman and a man is possible only if the woman has become the mother of a son and she transfers to her husband what she feels for her boy-child.

All this partakes of the same sociocultural models. But very few mythologists have explained the origins, the qualities and functions, the occasions and causes of disappearance of the great mother–daughter couples of mythology: Demeter–Kōrē, Clytemnestra–Iphigeneia and Jocasta–Antigone, to name only the best-known Greek figures.

To anyone who cares about social justice today, I suggest putting up posters in all public places with beautiful pictures representing the mother–daughter couple – the couple that illustrates a very special relationship to nature and culture. Such representations are missing from all civil and religious sites. This is a cultural injustice that is easy to remedy. There will be no wars, no dead, no wounded. This can be done before any reform of language, which will be a much longer process. This cultural restitution will begin to redress women's individual and collective loss of identity. It will cure them of some ills, including distress, but also rivalry, and destructive aggressiveness. It will help them move from the private sphere to the public, from the family to the society in which they live. The mother–daughter couple is always erased, even in places where a mother–daughter couple is honoured. Thus, the phenomenon of Lourdes – an event that attracts millions of pilgrims and tourists, involves many public gatherings and makes a great deal of money – concerns the relationship of a daughter to a so-called divine mother. Usually, however, the mother is represented without her daughter, most notably in churches, but also on street corners, and it is men who organize the worship, thus intervening in the relationship. But maybe this event commemorates the mother–daughter couple that was so important in the time before our patriarchal culture. Maybe – who knows? – it is a sign of things to come. In any case, it leaves no one indifferent.

We must not forget that in the time of women's law, the divine and the human were not separate. That means that religion was not a distinct domain. What was human was divine and became divine. Moreover, the divine was always related to nature. 'Supernatural' mother–daughter encounters took place in nature. Reintroduced into established religions, they are rarely interpreted from this none the less highly traditional perspective of women's religion. Why not? Subjected to the patriarchal churches for centuries, women have become sick of religion without giving any thought to their own divine traditions. Patriarchy has separated the human from the divine, but has also deprived women of their own gods or divinity(ies). Before patriarchy, women and men were potentially divine beings, which may mean social beings. In most traditions, all social organizations are chiefly religious. Religion gives the group cohesion. In a patriarchal regime, religion is expressed through rites of *sacrifice* or *atonement*. In women's history, religion is entangled with cultivation of the earth, of the body, of life, of peace. Religion became the opium of the people because it took over as the religion of mankind alone. It is actually a facet of the organization of society. But the deification, here and now, of sexual bodies is a different story: this exists in societies where women are not excluded from the organization of the culture. In India, for example, and at the beginning of our Greek culture – for to some extent this era still exists in India – sexuality was cultural, sacred. It was also an important source of energy for men and women. Patriarchy stripped women of divinity, taking it over in the places where men are amongst themselves, and often suspecting women's religion of devilry.

But few scholars or theologians have given any thought to the relationships of mother–daughter couples to fertility and respect for nature. After a certain era, women who were close to nature were called witches, practitioners of magic, whereas at the beginning of our History the mother–daughter couple was a positive representation of the site of worship of the body and the natural elements. Magic, holocausts and sacrificial or propitiatory rites did not come into play until after this relationship with nature was broken off – the only universal that could be both immediate and mediated with neither obscurity nor occultism.

Male religion masks an appropriation that interrupts the relationship with the natural universe and perverts its simplicity. It represents a social universe organized by men, but this organization is based on a sacrifice: the sacrifice of nature and the sexual body, particularly woman's. It imposes a spirituality cut off from its natural roots and environment and therefore cannot fulfil humanity. Spiritualization, socialization and cultivation must start with what is. Patriarchal regimes do not do so, because they seek to obliterate the means that they use to take control: (a) a wresting of power from the domain of the other sex and (b) excessive privilege for the family over the sexual couple.

Putting up images – photographs, paintings, sculptures, etc., not advertisements – of mother–daughter couples in all public places today would show respect for the social order. The social order is not made up of mothers and *sons*, as patriarchal culture represents it, with its own virginal ideals that it often assimilates to money, with its reproductive issues, with its incestuous games, and with its reduction of love to natural fertility, the release of social entropy, and so on.

Women's inability to organize themselves and agree on what they want makes some people smile and discourages others. But how could they unite when they have no representation, no example, of such an alliance? There was not always such a deficiency. At one time mother and daughter formed a natural and social model. The mother–daughter couple was the guardian of the fertility of nature in general, and of the relationship with the divine. In that era, food consisted of the fruits of the earth. The mother–daughter couple safeguarded human food and the site of oracular speech.

This couple preserved the memory of the past, and thus the daughter respected her mother, her ancestry. This couple was also concerned with the present: the earth produced food in peace and quiet. It was possible to foresee the future thanks to women's relationship with the divine, with oracular speech.

And were men harmed by this organizational structure? No. In respecting life, love and nature this way, neither sex was destroyed by the other. The two sexes loved each other without the institution of marriage, with no obligation to bear children – which never put an end to procreation – and with no censorship of sex or the body.

That is probably what monotheistic religions are telling us in the myth of earthly paradise, a myth that corresponds to centuries of History now called Prehistory, the primitive era, etc. The people of these so-called archaic times were perhaps more cultured than we are now. Traces of their artistry still remain: temples, sculptures and paintings, but also myths and tragedies, especially as expressions of the transition to the so-called historic era. The closest that this era came to our own time was the start of the Golden Age of Greece.

The beginnings of patriarchal power as we know it – which means the power of the man as the legal head of the family, tribe, people, state and so on – coincided with the separation of women from each other and especially the separation of daughters from their mothers. The mother–daughter relationship – the most fertile from the point of view of preserving life in peace – was destroyed to establish an order tied to private property, to the handing down of property within the male line of descent, to the institution of monogamous marriage so that property, including children, belong to this line of descent, and to the establishment of men-only social organizations for the same purpose.

★

2

My next examples will be drawn from the law. We must ask ourselves about the *written* representation of women's law. It is incredible but true that single-sexed theoretical and practical discourses can even exist, let alone be behind legislation. This has only been possible because women have been separated from their mothers, separated from each other and deprived of their own appropriate culture. To create a culture, it is necessary to gather together, talk to each other and organize without submission, dependency, or economic, legal, or religious prohibitions.

But women are still in a state of social and cultural subjugation, even those who believe they are free and emancipated. Why? Because the order that lays down the law is male. A few isolated gains have been made, but they have not changed much. Many people like to say that all women's struggles or feminist struggles are over. If so, that would mean that they never really existed, that what was at issue was poorly defined. Social and cultural sexualization for the two sexes is far from finished, and women's liberation can have no other issue.

I think that the main real condition of liberation that throngs of women have demanded is the right to contraception and abortion, and this is a right that a number of governments are ready to revoke. This right simply shows respect for women's lives and the fact that they are under no obligation to reproduce within their husband's line of descent. It must be combined with civil protection in the case of rape. It must also punish the assault and battery women suffer in private or public as an offence, and in some cases as a crime. These rights are essential to life and must be written into the law so that women are recognized as citizens.

The law has a sex, and justice has a sex, but by default.

(a) The law was written by mankind from a pro-slavery viewpoint as far as the difference between the sexes is concerned. The woman is supposed to leave her family, live with her husband, take his name, let herself be possessed by him physically, bear his children, bring them into the world, and raise them, which means nurture them, cook, wash, keep house – all boring, repetitive tasks like the ones that some people pity labourers for doing. Should anyone say that she benefits from the relationship because her husband works for her, I should answer that this division of labour, aside from keeping her a child (children are also fed by their parents and the state for doing the work that is scholastic learning), perverts her mentally to a much greater extent than workers are perverted by the benefits that capitalist industry and commerce produce for them. Being paid by their husbands makes women forget the respect and rights due their sex, their mothers, other women; today, it even makes them forget the concern for life. The difference between the sexes, to anyone who cares to examine this human dimension with a little objectivity, has been reduced to a question of money, like everything else.

(b) The second aspect of patriarchal law is that it deals almost exclusively with issues of property. The individual is defined ultimately by his or her relationship to ownership. He or she is subject to it. Because of its blindness to the significance of its patriarchal foundations, mankind no longer sees that the privilege of wealth originally concerns men alone. Politicians and theoreticians learnedly argue the fact that wealth, which is supposedly neutral, should be shared equitably by all. But wealth, understood as the accumulation of property through the exploitation of others, is already the result of the subjugation of one sex to the other. Capitalization is even the organizing force behind patriarchal power *per se*, through the mechanization of our sexually differentiated bodies and the injustice in dominating them.

Mankind has generally put property ahead of life. Men care little about living matter or its cultural economy. Men's society is built upon ownership of property. Life itself is treated like a commodity, productive capital, and possessed as a tool of labour, but not as the basis of an identity to be cultivated. Patriarchy cares little about spiritualizing sexually differentiated nature. This perverts its relationship to matter and its cultural organization. Hegel was particularly aware of this shortcoming of an ethics of our relationship to the natural world as it concerns the genders and their ancestries; Antigone is sacrificed because she pays her respects to the blood and gods of her mother by honouring her dead brother. Hegel wrote that this sacrifice hobbles the whole rest of the becoming of the spirit. Marx, on the other hand, was very concerned with social economy but little with the culture of nature, except in its transformation into useful goods, at which point it disappears as a natural phenomenon. We have thus been induced to talk a great deal about social justice, but in the process we have forgotten that it needed natural reserves and roots to survive. This is particularly obvious for women as reproducers, for raw materials, for arable soil, but it is also true of any body. No society can exist without its constituent bodies. This tautology is continually forgotten for reasons of male subjective economy, at least in our patriarchal cultures.

★

3

My third example concerns the question of the difference between men and women in subject–object and subject–subject relationships. Male society has characteristics which some people claim are universal, but which are in fact attributable to the sex of the people that compose it.

Thus, without a sexual culture, a (partially dialectical) pattern of cultural relations between the genders, man – in his logic, discourse, behaviour; his entire subjective economy – constantly oscillates between the *yes* and the *no* that he says to all forms of mothers in establishing his identity. The contradictions are manipulated in an increasingly anarchic fashion. Moreover, their pace escapes from whomever articulates them. Man needs these yesses and noes to maintain a distance between himself and the matter that produced him. More often than not, he seeks to remain in denial of this primary mother or matrix. His denial of reality is an attempt, by various means, including very subtle reasoning, to impose a *second nature* that eventually destroys the first or causes it to be forgotten. That is the culture or History of an era. Then, nature reasserts itself – provided there are any natural reserves left, which is questionable today. What is called human nature therefore often means forgetting or ignoring our corporeal condition for the sake of some spiritual delusion or perversion. And what exactly does 'human nature' denote? Surely it is a patriarchal working hypothesis, since this human nature does not consider sexual difference in defining a cultural identity. The obligation to have children or to keep house does not constitute a female identity. It is a function or social role, no more.

Woman's subjective identity is not at all the same as man's. She does not have to distance herself from her mother as he does – by a *yes* and especially a *no*, a *near* or a *far*, an *inside* opposed to an *outside* – to discover her sex. She is faced with another problem entirely. She must be able to identify with her mother as a woman to realize her own sexuality. She must be or become a woman like her mother and, at the same time, be able to differentiate herself from her. But her mother is the same as she. She cannot reduce or manipulate her as an *object* in the way a little boy or a man does. According to Freud, and theories of sexuality in general, our desire is a desire for objects, and for competition for objects. Violence is thus explained by this need to possess objects and the rivalry to take possession of them. A person's status and even identity is defined by the objects belonging to her or him. This economy is partially valid for male subjectivity. Woman, though, immediately becomes a subject with respect to another subject who is the same as she: her mother. She cannot reduce her mother to an object without reducing herself the same way, because they are of the same gender. Hence the all-or-nothing law of female desire if it does not find a subjective identity with respect to its mother. The *fort/da* that Freud describes as the child's entry into the world of language and culture does not work properly for the girl, except through identification with the boy. The little girl becomes alienated in someone other than herself and makes quasi-objects of her children and later sometimes of her husband. In this she may perhaps justify the phallic descriptions that are given of her. It is not her identity.

Confusing *identity* and *identification* is not the same thing as finding an order for the matter and form that we are. Confusing them is an idealistic delusion that produces a great deal of social entropy. That is where the neuter is often located: in the confusion between identity and identification. The delusion that they can obscurely be or become men, and vice versa, exiles women from themselves and makes them agents of individual and social destruction. But for all that, women are not in agreement or in harmony with themselves. The possible discovery of their identity, on the other hand, poses a major problem of subjective relationships. Woman has a direct intersubjective relationship with her mother. Hers is more an *inter-subject* economy than an economy of subject–object relations; it is thus a very social and cultural economy that has doubtless led to interpretations in which women are seen as the guardians of love. This subjective economy between mother and daughter can be partially translated into action, an objection pointed out by some women – or men – who for various reasons either deny or refuse to accept the necessity of a sex-specific discourse. But that is not enough. Woman must be able to express herself in words, images and symbols in this intersubjective relationship with her mother, then with other women, if she is to enter into a non-destructive relationship with men. This very special economy of woman's identity must be permitted, known and defined. It is essential to a real culture. It means supporting, not destroying, the mother–daughter relationship. It requires not believing that the daughter must turn away from her mother to obey her father or love her husband. For her to establish her own sexual identity, she needs a genealogical relationship with her own gender and respect for both genders. This respect is impossible without valid erotic models to replace neutralization of the sexes, or release, or desublimation, which are the models we see today.

★

4

What are our dominant sexual models? Male sexuality – there is no other, according to Freud – is constructed upon a model of energy involving tension, release and return to homeostasis. This economy obeys the two principles of thermodynamics long considered impossible to overcome. Sexuality is thus supposedly linked to physical laws that allow it no freedom or future other than a repetitive, explosive, non-evolutive one. The only way to escape this sad fate is through procreation.

Freud gives no indications about the process of sublimation in adulthood. Becoming men or women means simply becoming breeders; it does not mean acquiring a capacity for energy to think, share and cultivate with the other sex. According to this expert on sexuality, only partial drives can be sublimated. Does that mean that anyone who refuses to adhere to a reproductive genital model is subject to a theoretical and practical regression to partial drives?

What are these things called partial drives? Freud was interested chiefly in sight, but hearing, smell, taste and touch are also partial drives. Touch, which plays a role in all the senses, is a very special sense about which Freud says little. He is too preoccupied with objects. Touch is a more subjective, intersubjective sense; it is somewhere between active and passive; it escapes the possessive, mechanical and warlike economy, except when it is reduced to assault and battery or to a part of the body.

But what of this possible sublimation of our senses today? The energy involving tension, release and return to homoeostasis is competitive with technology, but as the return to equilibrium and stability is increasingly problematic, the energy seeks to become more and more intense, faster and faster. It must 'pulsate', it must 'explode', etc., and at any cost, otherwise it goes limp, it falls apart. These drives tend towards an increasingly strong release, according to a competitive model. But the escalation towards human and technological entropy makes us forget our condition as living beings. This pathos of increasing energy, of economic growth, both individual and collective, out of harmony with natural rhythms, sacrifices us little by little.

All these affects, these private or public feelings (often sustained by advertising in the service of commerce and industry without the knowledge of consumers, who are as passive as they are artificially impassioned), seem to be replacing a forgotten body. The body has much more of a relationship with *perception* than with *pathos*. A body breathes, smells, tastes, sees, hears and touches or is touched. These bodily attributes are endangered. But how can we live without bodies? What does this extinction mean? It means that men's culture has polluted our air, food, sight, hearing and touch to such an extent that our senses are on the verge of destruction. Yet we can neither live nor think without the mediation of our senses.

Doctors know that we are losing our hearing. Let us say that they confirm what experience and common sense should be teaching us. Our ears, constantly assaulted by the noise of machinery, including aircraft, no longer get any rest, and eventually become weaker in self-defence. They also suffer from the excessive speed and frequent changes in altitude to which we subject them in using our current modes of transportation. Yet out ears are our main organ of static equilibrium and of thermal and affective regulation. It is therefore impossible to ask people to be peaceful or civic-minded, much less affectionate, if they are constantly subjected to acoustic shock and tension. This is even truer of women, who are more sensitive than men from this point of view and who are no longer protected even at home, owing to the spread of technology and the growth of road and air traffic. Today, noise pollution and pollution of the other senses no longer affects just some types of workers, but the entire population, who receive no compensation in the form of wages or other benefits. In destroying our perceptions of sound, we are destroying a large part of our identity. Hearing is one of the senses awakened the earliest and the most passively (the foetus can hear inside the mother's womb), and the one that remains a component of the most advanced and most universal aspects of culture: oral communication and listening to music. It is therefore urgent to find an economy of noise that will protect our hearing. There are some very simple and ultimately inexpensive methods of doing so: restricting the number of roads for motor vehicles both inside and outside cities by creating many footpaths and quiet zones, not using the entire sky for airways, focusing research on the invention of quiet machinery. Some quiet machines already exist, and there are vital priorities to be respected, even if it means slowing down a little and teaching consumers to walk a bit more: in my view, these two changes are essential to their own lives, in any case.

As for our eyes, the glare of increasingly harsh and widespread public lighting is gradually wearing out their ability to accommodate, and the materials now used for windows in buildings, and especially in cars, make the reflection of sunlight harder and harder for us to bear. While the sellers of sun-glasses and their fellows are thriving, our bodies and our sensitivities are being destroyed.

I will not continue this sad enumeration. You all know that food often becomes insipid, if not toxic, as a result of chemical fertilizers, or growth accelerants, or livestock-raising methods. We have to go well out of the cities to be able to smell pleasant odours (although the sense of smell is essential to our vitality), aside from the fact that air, the most vital element, is polluted by many types of toxins to the point where its quality is at risk. Here again, although it is obviously right to denounce using the air as a weapon of death in time of war, I think that even more energy must be devoted to demanding breathable air for everyone in peacetime. Becoming attentive to certain risks should not mean becoming inattentive to the ongoing destruction of the body to which we are subjected. Especially since we no longer have any choice, or very little . . . Holiday spots, retreats and residential areas outside cities are also plagued by the noises of machinery, aircraft, four-by-four vehicles speeding up mountains, and motorbikes racing up and down country roads, hills, the seashore, rivers, and so on. The regulations governing when and where all this mechanized equipment, which is of doubtful utility, can be operated are very lax. Our society is extremely hypocritical in this regard: we decry young people's lack of upbringing or caution, but at the same time we provide them with machines capable of disturbing adults and causing accidents. In my opinion, the desire to earn and accumulate money means that only women who are aware of the danger and concerned about life can demand curbs on runaway technology in order to protect our mental and physical health. To do this, however, they must be vigilant, they must dare to speak up and say what they want, they must be able to express themselves publicly and make themselves heard.

Women do not obey the same sexual economy as men. I have already written a great deal on this subject. I can say again in a few words that their relationships to fluids and solids, to matter and form, to the sense of touch through skin and mucous membrane, to symmetry, to repetition, and so on, are all different. In this talk, I want above all to remind you that women do not have the same relationship to entropy, to homoeostasis, to release. Their internal regulation is much stronger, and it maintains them in a constant, irreversible process of growth. This is not necessarily negative; it is not necessarily a process of degeneration or accumulation. A woman reaches puberty, loses her virginity, is pregnant one or more times, reaches menopause, etc.; all these events mark a much more continuous temporality than do the ruptures of male sexuality or its continuum without irreversible momentum. Women's temporality is complex hormonally, and this has an effect on the body's organization and general equilibrium. But each moment of this becoming has its own specific, often cyclical, temporality linked to cosmic rhythms. If women have felt so threatened by the Chernobyl accident, it is because their bodies have this irreducible relationship to the universe. This component of their sexually specific becoming does not mesh well with the acceleration towards which technology is drawing us. A pregnancy has a fixed term, just as menstruation has a cycle. Women are thus under the constraints of a *dual temporality*. In some places, it is touching and anachronistic to see a pregnant women. Society none the less requires them to be pregnant, and the medical assistance they receive does not alleviate the affective, nervous and hormonal problems that they encounter. What is more, while the need for the interventions of the medical establishment must certainly be acknowledged, when medical procedures become essential and standard as a result of the pace of life and all the various forms of pollution, they strip women of their responsibility and contribute to a loss of identity.

I know that women's relationship to a natural temporality means that they are sometimes considered to be a brake on culture, to be 'reactionary', and that they actually consider themselves to be so. I personally disagree with this interpretation. Chernobyl proves it, and so do many other phenomena, some of which I have described. We need regulation that is in keeping with natural rhythms; we need to cultivate this natural filiation, and not destroy it in order to impose upon it a split, dual nature of our bodies and our elemental environment. Women are affected more fatally by the break with cosmic equilibria. It is therefore up to them to say *no*. Without their *yes*, the world of men cannot continue to develop or subsist. Women must learn when to say *no*, and why; they must also know how to say it. This requires them to become fully conversant with the subjectivity–objectivity relationship – a learning experience that women are particularly lacking as a result of their cultural past of identification with the object of desire. Women can acquire this knowledge. It must be included in the political and cultural syllabus for girls. I shall now give you a little example of a possible way to distance ourselves from an authority that imposes its laws on us, and to distance oneself from oneself as a listening and speaking subject.

★

5

I am taking this example because it is a good idea to know how to analyse a discourse, rather than listen to it credulously or passively, and to learn to identify the sex of the person speaking and that person's relationship to the other sex and to the world, on the basis of very simple linguistic and logical theories.

Of course, we must first remember that language is not neutral and that its rules weigh heavily on the constitution of a female identity and on women's relationships with one another.

What does it mean to say that language is not neutral? First, a few very simple things [bearing in mind that in French any noun is masculine, feminine, or neuter, and that any adjective, participle, pronoun, etc., used with it accordingly also takes the masculine, feminine, or neuter form; and taking note of which nouns are neuter]. (a) The plural of the two genders together is always masculine; 'Électeurs, électrices, vous êtes tous des Ital*iens*' [Voters (men and women), you are all Italian (masculine plural)]; to be 'Ital*iennes*' [feminine plural], you would have to be a group of women only; (b) the most valorous realities are usually masculine in our patriarchal cultures: *le Dieu* [God], *le soleil* [the sun], etc.; (c) the neuter, which often takes the place of a sexual difference that has been erased, is expressed in the same form as the masculine; this is true of natural phenomena (*il tonne*, *il vente*, *il fait soleil*, etc.) [it is thundering, it is windy, it is sunny] or realities involving an obligation or a right (*il faut*, *il est nécessaire*, etc.) [it must, it is necessary]. These forms of language and speech that seem to us to be universal, true, intangible, are in fact determined and modifiable historical phenomena. They entail consequences for the content of discourse that are different for each sex. I have been analysing statements by men and women and have begun to interpret these differences. It would take too long to tell you the findings today. They will be published soon.[1] But, because we are meeting after Chernobyl and with a view to meditating on the accident that occurred there, I would like to tell you that I have analysed, among other things, certain speeches on nuclear weapons given by men in international political situations. This scientific work proves that when we do more than just listen in our usual, naive manner, we find that these political pleas are often devoid of any content. It is true that the emptier the discourse, the greater our tendency to project something into it. Nothingness disturbs us, frightens us, remains foreign to us. But I think that those who make these speeches are themselves unaware of how little sense they make and of their own lack of subjective freedom and responsibility. They are just as confused as we are, if not more so, although they may not want to admit it, even to themselves. I propose that we try to break away from this fascination with emptiness, not by being aggressive or vengeful, but rather through rigorous analysis of discourses that decree or discuss social and political laws. This would show that fictitious realities and an inertia of linguistic rules structure much political discourse, and in particular that abstract *inanimate* concepts are substituted for *animate* subjects. Political discourse thus has a sort of magical economy. 'Progress', 'social justice', 'peace', 'conflicts', 'weapons', etc., are not people actively responsible for social and historical developments, but supposedly neutral concepts or notions that men (sometimes women, through mimicry) use in order to release themselves from their subjectivity, their relationship to their interlocutors, their responsibility to the world, in an abstract evolution that has little orientation in space and time. Should anyone object that this is merely the style of political discourse, I should answer that this has not always been the case, but that contemporary leaders seem to be trapped in the language and culture they have produced as if caught in a net or sinking in quicksand. They are prisoners of their own civilization.

But while some men (and women) have chosen violence as a means of expression, often out of despair, speeches that mean nothing also call, in their own way, for recourse to violence, to war, as a way to set limits on non-meaning, on nothingness. Speaking but saying nothing, especially in the context of a political mandate, entails the risk that exchanges between countries, between persons, will be expressed otherwise than through words. It also opens up the possibility that a dictatorial 'I' may appropriate energy without effective, responsible people to decree and apply its truth.

The sacrifice of the natural spirit, of the spirit of the female gender in particular, and of a certain sense of the family spirit to the neutrality of citizens devoted to serving the state, science, or technology has substituted the social blindness of men-amongst-themselves – libidinal blindness, a blindness of arguments, ideas and perspectives cut off from their concrete content – for vital, material routedness. This blindness assumes and accelerates forgetting, wilful ignorance, destruction of the sensible world, when we need to find an objective and subjective articulation between nature and culture.

What would I advise women to do to create a discourse that is neither seductive nor reductive?

(a) Never abandon subjective experience as an element of knowledge. The most transcendental theory is also rooted in subjective experience. The truth is always produced by someone. That does not mean that it contains no objectivity.

(b) Do not indulge in public displays of spontaneity or impulsiveness: naive sentiments, aggressiveness, etc. This attitude is the other side of the belief in a truth independent of the subject; this is how the existing culture has blinded women.

(c) Constantly work on a dialectic between subjectivity and objectivity. Patriarchal civilization, apart from our own relationship with the natural world, has put us in the position of objects; we must learn to become subjects capable of speech.

(d) Do not subscribe or adhere to the existence of a neutral, universal science, which women would have difficulty entering, and which they would use to repress themselves and other women, transforming science into a new superego. This is a mystification of the innocence of feelings, but also of scientific truth. All truth is partially relative. A theoretical truth that forces us to abandon all subjective reference points is dangerous.

★

6

This brings me to the last point of my talk. I shall not develop it very far, since I wanted to highlight the practical aspects of cultural transformation towards greater justice and therefore chose to limit myself to certain fields of knowledge or science. The point, which will be my conclusion, is this: Do all our sciences and fields of knowledge present themselves in a neutral, universal manner? My answer is no. How could they? Any knowledge is produced by subjects in a given historical context. Even if it tends towards objectivity, even if its techniques are supposed to be means of controlling objectivity, science is the manifestation of certain choices, certain exclusions, essentially because of the sex of the scientists. Some epistemologists now have an idea of the impact that the subject has on the object examined, and especially studied, by the sciences. But their enquiry almost always stops short of interpreting the influence of the subject's sex. This division between sex and theory is very old. It can be explained by resistance surrounding seizure of power and a very restricted and repressive concept of sexuality.

After hearing the summary of some of my analyses of various sectors of the humanities and social sciences, I think you will understand that the following facts are not unrelated to the sex and history of the scientific subject.

(a) Today this subject is extremely interested in acceleration exceeding our human possibilities, weightlessness, travelling through natural space and time, overcoming cosmic rhythms and their regulations, but also in disintegration, fission, explosion, catastrophes, and so on. This reality can be verified in the natural sciences and humanities.

– Freud defines the identity of the subject as *Spaltung*, but this term also refers to nuclear fission. Nietzsche, too, perceived his ego as an atomic nucleus threatening to explode. And in my opinion, the chief problem that Einstein poses is that he leaves us no other chance but his God, given his interest in acceleration without electromagnetic rebalancing. Of course, he played the violin; music preserved his own personal equilibrium. But what does this general relativity that lays down the law outside of nuclear power plants, and that challenges our corporeal inertia, a necessary condition of life, mean to us?

– Astronomer Hubert Reeves, in keeping with the American Big Bang theory, describes the origin of the universe as an explosion. Why this current interpretation so consistent with the descriptions of other theoretical discoveries?

– René Thom, another theoretician at the crossroads between science and philosophy, speaks of catastrophe through conflict, rather than generation through abundance, growth and positive attractions, especially natural ones.

– Specialists in quantum mechanics are interested in the disappearance of the world.

– Scientists today are working on increasingly imperceptible particles that can be defined only with technical instruments and energy beams.

– Freud and, after him, Marcuse were very pessimistic about the chances of life drives. But death drives are an individual and collective instrument of disintegration and decomposition.

– Philosophers take a keen interest in the deconstruction of ontology, in the ante- and the post-, but little interest in the constitution of a new, rationally founded identity.

– Sociologists break us down into fragments of identity, semiologists into sememes, pertinent traits, functions, etc.

– And the master psychoanalysts and their descendants generally refuse to consider that discourse has a sex. How then is sexuality expressed if not through language? What are these learned practitioners doing to us when they state one truth on the one hand, another truth on the other: there is a sexual difference, but not a sexuality of discourse?

– To neurologists this translates as: the brain has a sex, but language does not, or if it does, it is not our problem.

Where, then, in all these disintegrations, explosions, splits, or multiplicities, these losses of corporeal identity, are we to find our subjective status? Of course, men are struggling with the absolute that they have created. After a preparatory course rigorously repressive of truth, the duty to remember the past, respect for the father and for God as Father, the shift from quantitative to qualitative, they suggest to us methods such as 'chance', 'accident', 'ignorance', 'multiplicity', 'pluralism', 'breaks' with the past, 'forgetting', 'leaps', 'murders of the father', etc. Science and knowledge today consist in an education in the negative without a positive horizon, a sort of onto-theology without God, except to some scholars. But how do they articulate their knowledge, their God, and a human ethics?

Are we not faced with an explosion or release of overly saturated or overly entropic theoretical models, with a considerable risk to human bodies and minds?

(b) This sort of cultural semi-release is often accompanied by an acceleration of theoretical and practical contradictions, an ever-increasing estrangement from our corporeal matter and its properties, a search for self in abstraction or dream, an unthought-of gap between the technological environment, its influence upon us and ideological entropies that cannot be counter-balanced, in my opinion, except by cultivating our *sexual* bodies.

(c) Most scientists have lost control of their discoveries; either they no longer perceive what they themselves are doing, but are acting as intermediaries in the development of theories or techniques they have not produced, or they are so out of touch with philosophy, our everyday wisdom, that they no longer think. With microscopes or macroscopes in hand, scientists forget their bodies, forget life. According to Plato this was already true in his time. But it is more dangerous for us today. And it is not funny any more . . . The epistemology of science has fallen far behind technological development and its effects.

★

I shall stop now for today. You may have been expecting me to develop this last point further. Here, with you and after Chernobyl, I wanted to talk about human realities that require rapid changes and about the contribution you can make to these changes. I did not feel it would be ethical to work out a more subtle epistemological theory without proposing simple and effective cultural changes that give us a chance to live. That is the theme of your festival, and I am in full agreement.

Living requires knowing how to stop, reflect, and even contemplate, so that we can become capable of situating ourselves individually and collectively. It is an essential condition for arriving at a fair decision concerning social and cultural measures. We need them now to slow down a worldwide escalation towards economic and cultural entropy. Women must demand, and take, these measures in a way that respects their bodies and their freedoms.

Notes to Chapter 1: A Chance to Live

1 Luce Irigaray with Rachel Bers *et al.*, *Sexes et genres à travers les langues: éléments de communication sexuée* (Paris: Grasset, 1990)–Tr.

2

HOW DO WE BECOME CIVIL WOMEN?

Rome, 8 April 1988
Preparation for the panel 'Women's Time' [*Il tempo delle donne*]
Women of the PCI and the magazine Reti

2

How do we Become Civil Women?

In *Speculum*,[1] I wrote that to re-establish a political ethics a dual dialectic is necessary, one for the male subject and another for the female subject (pp. 223–4). Today I would say that a triple dialectic is necessary: one for the male subject, one for the female subject, and one for their relationship as a couple or in a community.

The weak and strong point of this quest concerns the issue of subjectivity and objectivity for women.

The world today is in the throes of an identity crisis. I think it augurs well for the Italian Communist Party that it is becoming aware of this crisis, especially where justice for women is concerned. That is why I am here, in the hope of making a few suggestions for intellectual mediation that will help us to escape from this upheaval in identity.

Carrying them out assumes a twofold effort on the part of women. It is cruel but true that, in the period of History we are going through, women must make a much greater effort than men. But what is at stake is worth the effort: it is a concern for life and its culture.

Women's twofold effort consists in interpreting their

current situation or status not only in economic but also in symbolic terms. They must realize that it is just as important for them to keep or acquire their subjective and objective status as simply to enter into existing economic or cultural systems. Unless they realize that they are members of two groups – women and units of the contemporary world – they risk losing everything without achieving recognition despite all their efforts.

Analysing this twofold reference today requires a great deal of patience from women who are working and women who are trying to think, think about themselves; sometimes they are one and the same, incidentally. No sooner have they been accepted as participants in group work than they must conduct a self-analysis to make sure that they do not submit to laws other than those possible for them.

This is a considerable task – not generally rewarded; penalized, rather – but necessary. Neglecting it or carrying it out blindly can be quite disruptive of today's political community, particularly amongst women.

So I would like to share with you some of my thoughts – also the result of ongoing self-analysis, sometimes prompted by meetings with various groups of women – in an attempt to solve a number of problems at the crossroads of the individual and the collective, a crossroads that is being examined in various societies today. This examination has led some women and men to turn inwards and take an individual position, and others to blend into or lose themselves in a collective 'we' or 'they' that does not seem to be an adequate response to the world's political necessities.

I have four types of suggestion to make.

(1) The first suggestions concern the development of

the subjective status of girls and boys in their relationship to their first sexual partner, their mother.

(2) I shall then talk about job titles for women, an issue with which you are already familiar.

(3) I shall briefly analyse the sex-specific dimension of objects or property possessed by men and women.

(4) I shall then suggest some concrete legal changes that would give women a civil identity. These changes are necessary both for the sake of elementary social justice and in order to re-establish a minimum of legal consistency.

For what do women's work and political affiliation mean if women have not got their own civil identity? Will they not be supporting and promoting a male tradition and society to which they remain alien, and which, to some extent, annihilates them as persons?

This change of legal definition in the strict sense must go hand in hand with a linguistic change. The organization of the law reflects that of the language and vice versa. Today there are an increasing number of cases, to some extent heterogeneous and contradictory, in both the law and language that cannot be resolved by an appeal to a neutral individual. At the same time, a lack of appropriate human rights can be seen in many crimes, such as private or public violence against women and their property, rape in the strict sense of the word, pornographic trade conducted without a consenting decision by women as responsible individuals, involuntary prostitution, kidnapping of children, incest (sometimes followed by abortion forced on teenagers), or any use of their bodies by their fathers, brothers, uncles, or other members of the family, and so on.

These shortcomings of the law are strangely parallel

to those of language and speech with respect to the identity of the injured parties. Thus, twice the harm is done, and there is no possible recourse.

1 *Development of the Primary Relationship to the Mother and Sexual Identity*

As children, we are borne by a woman, nurtured by *her*, mothered by *her*. Some of these functions are made necessary by nature (conception itself, carrying the child, giving birth, breast-feeding, etc.), others by culture, at least in part, e.g. mothering. But in most cases, the first interlocutrix of the child, whether boy or girl, is *elle* [she], the mother. *Il* [he] is there, but a relationship between him and the child is either impossible (*in utero*, for example) or extremely limited (mothering).

And yet the language we call our mother tongue reverses things now: *il* [he] and *ils* [they; masculine] are present everywhere; *elle* is almost always erased, because all agreements of masculine and feminine together are masculine. And it is not just a question of the agreement of subject personal pronouns, which are less of a problem in Italian than in French because they are not necessarily expressed, but of all the grammatical agreements involving other pronouns, participles, adjectives, demonstratives, articles, etc. To use *elle*, you must be speaking of a woman alone in a social activity, a situation which almost never occurs, and for which the language lacks a vocabulary and grammatical rules. I shall come back to this in points two and three.

Why does a woman have to be alone and engaged in social activity (beyond the context of marriage, it would be wise to add) for *elle* to be kept? Because everything collective in social life is expressed using the masculine plural. But in private life, family life, supposedly the quintessential women's domains, there is no feminine gender either, except in the primary relationship to the mother. By that I mean that a couple is talked about in the masculine plural because it is formed of *il* + *elle*, and *il* + *elle* = *ils*. The feminine of a married woman thus becomes *il(s)*. Furthermore, a family is always designated by the masculine plural because it is composed of husband and wife, or father and mother, and child(ren). No representation of the family allows the use of *elle*, the first interlocutrix of the child subject. This *elle* is erased even in the community of marriage and family (whether institutional or not). So baby girls and boys have no way of designating their mother as *elle*. As soon as they enter into the linguistic order, they mourn the loss of *elle*. This has several consequences.

(a) The boy loses his (specifically female interlocutrix. No more feminine *tu* [you; singular/familiar] for him. Henceforth all valid interlocutors will be *il(s)*. Language and society, society and language will have it thus. This absence of the feminine as a gender representing half of all interlocutors leads to a failure to identify women as subjects who can be addressed. The feminine no longer has any status as an existing valid interlocutrix. Women are entities or things, earth, depths, reserves which give birth, mother, do housework, with whom one makes love, etc., but not partners in discourse. Even seduction, supposedly the operation of a – more or less diabolical – subject, actually involves methods derived from commerce and social conventions adapted, as silently as possible, to the universe of men-amongst-themselves [*l'entre-ils*].

If the boy-child thus mourns the loss of his mother as a partner, the man mourns the loss of his woman partner. According to the laws of language, men keep to themselves, amongst fathers and sons or amongst brothers. To maintain a grammatical *elle*, a human *elle*, the right to virginity without maternity must be restored. Only a girl's virginal identity would remain in the feminine. Our cultures sense this to such an extent that the most divine female symbol, Mary, is represented as the virgin mother of a son. Mary plus Jesus makes another *ils*. What remains *elle* is a virgin girl. Another necessary change: restore female ancestries and communities of women. Then *elles* can be kept. From this point of view, it should be emphasized that the Anne → Mary line of descent, preliminary to the birth of the one called the Messiah, is obliterated today from most forms of Christian worship. It is not generally known that Mary, like Jesus, is said to have been conceived without sin. This gives another meaning to her virginity, notably with respect to her own mother: to her *elle*, to their *elles*.

(b) For what happens from the point of view of the girl according to our symbolic codes? She loses her sexual identity. That means that she loses the maternal *elle* and the *elle* of her own identity. No more feminine *tu* for her, the daughter; no more feminine *je* [I], either. The daughter loses her relationship to an interlocutrix of her own gender, to a *tu* of her own gender, and to a subject, a *je*, of her own gender. As a woman, she is excluded from the systems of intersubjective communication, outside the verbal exchanges that are relationships amongst *ils*, amongst representatives of the masculine gender. If she is to say *elle*, she must be taught, despite language and society, to maintain her mother as *elle* and to define herself or keep herself as *elle* with respect to other women. Otherwise she must identify with the masculine gender.

There are two very serious consequences, then, of the dominance of the masculine plural. The boy and man no longer have an interlocutrix (interlocutrices), and the girl and woman no longer have a linguistic subject or interlocutrix (interlocutrices). The world of discourse revolves around *ils*, which results in severe pathologies in the status of subjectivity and relations of communication. To put it bluntly, real persons are not represented or are represented other than according to their sex. This disrupts the definition of subjects and objects of communication.

In psychoanalytical terms, the boy does not resolve his Oedipus complex, as they say, at least in our languages. Neither does the girl. Language leaves men amongst themselves and deprives women of women-amongst-themselves [*l'entre-elles*]. Linguistic order does not allow a dilemma. It devalues the feminine generically. It overvalues the masculine.

To determine the effect of these grammatical rules on the speaking subject, I gave groups of secondary school and university students little language tests. More specifically, I asked teachers I know, women and men (unfamilar with my work) to give them. The tests were given orally, while the answers were written, for the most part. I myself gathered a few oral responses, which were a little different, but not on the points that I want to talk about. So far I have analysed the results from about 150 women and 100 men.[2] But I have given a great many overlapping tests that can be cross-checked. Similar tests are currently being studied for Italian, English and Dutch, and soon will be for Japanese, Greek and German. The purpose is to examine the manifestation of the sexes and the differences between them in various languages and cultures, and the possible movements between them. A preliminary work comparing French, Italian and English will soon be published in French in a collection titled *Sexes et genres à travers les langues*.[3]

The following facts regarding possible or impossible relationships between the sexes have already been confirmed by my findings from these little language tests:

– Men designate themselves or other men as subjects of a sentence. This appears either explicitly in proper nouns or pronouns, or in the syntactical organization and grammatical markers of the sentence.

– Men talk to each other, communicate amongst themselves, but do not address women much except when the message content puts women in a mothering role (for example, men sometimes complain to *elle* [her] rather than to *lui* [him] or *eux* [them; masculine]). This can be seen in the way the interlocutor is designated and the reasons for or topics of conversation.

– Women seldom designate themselves or other women as subjects of speech. They much more frequently put men in the position of subjects of the statement.

When women use *je* as the subject of a sentence, this woman *je* most often addresses a man and not another woman or women. It does not relate to itself either (for example, 'Je m'interroge' [I wonder], 'Je me regarde pour moi-même' [I look at myself for myself], 'Je me recueille' [I meditate], 'Je me touche' [I touch myself], etc.).

This type of response shows the trouble women have:

(a) representing themselves

(b) establishing a dialectic with themselves as empirical subjects

(c) respecting their mothers and other women as other than themselves

(d) providing models, plans, ideals, divinities, etc., for themselves. Most women take it badly when some women do so. They feel that we should remain empirical subjects, earthing masculine heads, that we should become masculine heads, unless we stick to a sort of undifferentiated and impersonal *on* [one, we] that is more or less dominated by male ideals.

These speech habits, which are clear from the responses gathered, pose serious ethical questions. Men are practically the only subjects and the only interlocutors in verbal exchanges. The act of taking women's place to earn money, to run society, has been accompanied by the appropriation of rules and standards of speech to suit men's needs and desires. This is not at all surprising. To trade produce or products, or to govern citizens, symbolic laws are necessary. Since men were assigned to these tasks, they appropriated the laws.

The assignment of reproduction and housekeeping to women did not require them to have a very elaborate linguistic code, especially after children began to be educated at school. The language of the female subject was thus reduced to the minimum. Women were induced to speak of others – men and children – and not of themselves. Their conversation concerned immediate, concrete things, to do with preparing food and running the household, for instance. In relationships with one another, the only things that mattered were dressing to be attractive and issues of childbirth and bringing up small children.

These facets of the language are still evident in women's speech, and they cannot be ignored in a culture where most conversations are no longer rooted in reality because of their repetitions of a vanished past or their abstractions that lose sight of theme and interlocutor alike.

Men's speech primarily concerns competitive techniques of producing consumable and exchangeable goods (even in most leisure time). It is little concerned with the culture of the sexual subject that is the male speaker. Becoming a man seems to correspond to distancing oneself from oneself, from one's concrete, living environment, entering into a coded universe that more or less accurately duplicates reality, acquiring the skills to compete, wage war, etc. Fortunately there are exceptions to these norms, but social and linguistic rules maintain them through a whole system of habits and value assignments.

In comparison with these properties of men's speech, the women's sentences that I gathered and analysed show subjective and objective values that should be preserved.

– Women attach much more importance to their relationship to the *other sex*, while men keep to themselves. Beyond the rules of society and language, their speech indicates an attraction to relations with the other sex that I feel is tied to a life culture.

– In general, women are much more interested in *others*. This can be seen, for example, in the use of transitive verbs with a person as the animate object – 'Je le lave' [I wash him], 'M'aimes-tu?' [Do you love me?] – or of prepositions expressing intersubjectivity; *avec* [with], *entre* [between, amongst], à [to], *pour* [for], etc.

– Women are more attentive to the question of *place*: they are close to things, to others (*autres*, which is related to one of the Indo-European roots of the verb *être* [to be]).

– Women care more about the *qualities* of people, things, actions. Their speech contains more adjectives and adverbs than men's does. This brings up a very interesting linguistic problem regarding women's speech in earlier times.

– Women are more interested in the *present* and the *future*, and men in the past.

– Women are more concerned with the *message* to be transmitted than are men. Women always try hard to say something. Men let inertia carry them or stick to wordplay unless their message expresses their moods.

Some components of women's speech must therefore be kept, while others must be acquired. Indeed, women's access or return to group work, to public places, to social relationships, requires linguistic changes. The obligation to review the rule requiring the mixed plural to be expressed in the masculine is an example. And if anyone objects that it is impossible to change this rule, and that in any case it is unimportant – since the masculine represents the 'neutral' (?) term, the 'unmarked' (?) gender – I suggest that the following law be passed: The mixed plural will be masculine one year; feminine the next. The effects of this genuinely democratic process should be analysed in order to alter the inertia of linguistic norms.

2 *Job Titles for Women*

Another obvious example of the current inadequacy of the language can be seen in how difficult it is to name women's occupational status. Job titles have become such a major issue because they lie halfway between subject and object. It is truly a case of *possessing* occupational status, of *having* a job and money, but this property cannot be possessed like any other object. It is part of the subjective identity, although it is not enough to constitute it. Moreover, this demand is easily combined with social demands that already exist in the male world. The issue is therefore relatively easy to articulate. It meets with almost universal acceptance. Often the only opposition it meets is in the case of realities that are already linguistically coded (for example, *moissonneuse* [mechanical harvester] and *cafetière* [coffee-pot] denote objects, and cannot be extended to people [woman harvester or woman coffee-shop owner], without unsatisfactory connotations). Social resistance of another type usually depends on the level of access permitted or denied to women. This can lead to some rather amusing linguistic anomalies, and I would like to read you an example. (It is an obituary taken from the newspaper *L'Indépendant* of 3 September 1987. A linguist looking for examples of current usage passed it on to me.)

> Nicole Chouraqui, ancien secrétaire général adjoint du R.P.R., député européen, maire adjoint de Paris est décédée à son domicile parisien à l'âge de quarante-neuf ans des suites d'un cancer.
>
> Née à Alger le 18 mars 1938, cette économiste de formation, après une carrière d'analyste financier à la

banque de l'Union parisienne de 1960 à 1966, s'était engagée dans la vie politique en adhérent au Parti radical. En 1970, elle rejoint le R.P.R., dont elle sera membre du bureau politique jusqu'en 1977, puis secrétaire général adjoint en 1978. Secrétaire national chargée du travail, de 1981 à 1984, elle est élue député européen en 1979 et réélue en 1984.

Conseiller de Paris dans le XIXe arrondissement, adjoint au maire Jacques Chirac, elle était aussi conseiller régional d'Ile-de-France. Mariée à l'assureur Claude Chouraqui, elle était mère de deux filles.

Nicole Choraqui, former deputy general secretary of the Rassemblement pour la République [Rally for the Republic: RPR], member of the European Parliament, and deputy mayor of Paris, has died at her home in Paris at the age of 49, of cancer.

Born in Algiers on 18 March 1938, she was an economist by training. After a career as a financial analyst with the Banque de l'Union parisienne [Bank of the Parisian Union], from 1960 to 1966, she entered political life by joining the Parti radical [Radical Party]. In 1970, she joined the RPR, and was a member of the party executive until 1977, becoming deputy general secretary in 1978. National labour secretary from 1981 to 1984, she was elected to the European Parliament in 1979 and re-elected in 1984.

She was a Paris city councillor for the 19th arrondissement and deputy mayor under Jacques Chirac, as well as a regional councillor for Ile de France. She was married to insurer Claude Chouraqui and had two daughters.

This example concerns the obituary of a woman politician. I think it is significant. For a woman *alone* to be spoken of in this way, maybe she has to die. Who knows? In this little notice, everything regarding the identity strictly permitted to a woman is in the feminine, while the rest is in the masculine. So Nicole Chouraqui:

– died [*est décédée*] at her home in Paris at the age of 49

– was born [*née*] in Algiers on 18 March 1938

– was married [*mariée*] to insurer Claude Chouraqui

– had two daughters (hurray for 'daughter' and not 'child'); attitudes are changing!).

But the rest of this short piece is full of grammatical anomalies, inconsistencies in the use of gender that show that we are in the midst of a transition on this issue.

Nicole Chouraqui was thus the 'ancien secrétaire général adjoint au R.P.R.' [former deputy general secretary of the RPR; masculine] and not the 'ancien*ne* secrétaire général*e* adjoint*e* au R.P.R.'. Is it because she herself or the RPR already has 'une secrétaire générale adjointe', i.e. a stenographer-typist-cum-computer operator, undoubtedly of the feminine gender? Or is it because the post of 'secrétaire général adjoint' of the RPR is almost always occupied by a man and it would be practically sacrilegious to feminize the title of this lofty position? These alternatives are actually two sides of the same question of the different values assigned to the masculine and feminine genders.

If I continue to read this piece, I see that Nicole Chouraqui was a 'député européen' [MEP; masculine] and not '"députée" européen*ne*' [feminine] or 'député "européen*ne*"'. Yet *député* is actually a nominalized past participle. It could easily be put back into its grammatical category and written in the feminine. But if it remains a masculine substantive, can the accompanying adjective be written in the feminine to designate a woman?

To continue: Nicole Chouraqui is 'cet*te* économiste de formation', and the economist by training can remain in the feminine. On the other hand,

> après une carrière d'*analyste financier* à la banque de l'Union parisienne de 1960 à 1966, [elle] s'était engagé*e* dans la vie politique en adhérant au Parti radical. En 1970, elle rejoint le R.P.R., dont elle [devient] secrétaire généra*l* adjoin*t* en 1978.

So we find the masculine used when it is a question of access to professional life and legitimate political positions. Women as women may pursue training as an economist, but not a career as a financial analyst or deputy general secretary of a party.

To continue: Though 'secrétaire national' (in the masculine), she may nevertheless be, and I quote, 'chargé*e* du travail, de 1981 à 1984' in the feminine! I repeat, 'Secrétaire national chargé*e* du travail, de 1981 à 1984, elle est élue député européen en 1979 et réélue en 1984'. Grammatical agreement really needs rethinking. If Nicole Chouraqui was 'secrétaire chargée du travail', why was she not 'secrétaire national*e*', for example? In short, this little piece, which is certainly trying to be rigorous, gives us an amusing demonstration of the current difficulty in applying the grammatical code concerning gender and of the need for it to evolve. The issue is not style, which may vary from one publication to another, but a problem of linguistic rules and usage.

3 The Sex of Objects and Property

Female subjects and their occupational qualifications are still poorly represented in language. In the Romance languages, the value of the feminine cannot be balanced out by the appropriation of property or objects. In Italian or in French, the difference between the sexes is not immediately obvious in terms of the object possessed, the way it is in English or German, for example. In our Romance languages, the possessive takes the gender of the object and not that of the possessor. We say: 'il ou elle voyage avec *sa* voiture' [he or she drives his/her car]: 'il ou elle embraces *son* enfant' [he or she hugs his/her child]: 'il ou elle a écrit *son* livre dans *sa* maison' [he or she wrote his/her book in his/her house]. While an English-speaking feminist can be satisfied with having *her* husband (as he has *his* wife), having bought *her* house, having won *her* university post, having written *her* book, etc., the same does not apply to us, whose language is more stratified with regard to the subject. This means that subject–object relationships are much more complex and that things and words themselves have sexual properties as subjects.

Today it is fashionable to say that the gender of words is arbitrary, totally unrelated to the question of sex. It is not true. One way or another, the gender of words is related to the question of the gender of the speaking subjects. Words have a sort of hidden sex, and this sex is unequally valued depending on whether it is masculine or feminine. This fact is not always immediately perceptible, and extensive synchronic and diachronic studies of the lexis are often necessary to make it apparent. Research of this type reveals that the gender of a word can be explained by, for instance:

- a forgotten sexual identification
- a semantic root that somehow evokes a sexual identity
- a prefix or suffix related to an action or state that is attributed to one sex rather than the other
- the time when the word became fixed in the language and the relative value of the sexes at that time
- the language of origin.

Some attributions of gender to words seem clearly linked to an identification of the reality denoted and the sex of the subject. In our Romance cultures, the sun has become the symbol of man, of the man-god: he is the sun or the sun is him. The moon thus represents the female, the man-god's sister. The earth is also called the sister or the mother) and the sky is the brother (or the father), etc. Traces of this sort of identification often remain in the gender of words. And at some point the masculine gender became the more valorous because it was supposed to represent the celestial and its spiritual qualities.

There is a mechanism at play other than identification between the reality denoted and sex:

- living, animate, human, cultivated beings become masculine
- lifeless, inanimate, non-human, uncultivated objects become feminine.

As a result, men have become the only social subjects, and women are assimilated to objects of exchange amongst them.

The status of word gender appears to be related to patriarchal cultures defined by the exchange of women amongst men, domination of the family by the father and patrilineality (or the matrilineal avunculate that preceded it), and appropriation by the father-man of property: land, tools, house, art, language, gods, heaven, etc. The patriarch thus possesses women and tools as goods often marked by the feminine gender. Even the maternal function, both natural and spiritual, is assimilated to the establishment of the power of men's father-gods through appropriation of female virginity. Thus Athena is the virgin who is the spiritual protector of the new Greek polis of men-amongst-themselves, and Mary is the virgin mother who gives birth to the Son of Man. These events coincide, unfortunately, with the disappearance of divine female lines of descent and social relationships between women. They mark the inception of a time when woman became a thing and the things useful to man became of the feminine gender. This is one of the reasons why women's job titles are often a problem: the feminine of the masculine term has become the thing belonging to the man (a *moissonneur* [harvester; masculine] is a man, while a *moissonneuse* [mechanical harvester; feminine] is a tool used by man) [see p. 27].

The difficulty involved in using this word to name a woman's occupation is thus threefold:

– A man holds on to the gender of the tool which takes his sexual partner's place.

– A woman does not want a title that is personally

disparaging, yet what is proposed is the name of a thing or the name of a person with a pejorative suffix, e.g. *doctoresse*.

– How can a woman be put to work with a machine that has taken her place?

These questions are thus complex both in terms of language and of socioeconomic status. When a linguist or law-maker claims that the masculine is a sort of neuter gender independent of the sex of the subjects, he is wrong. There are indeed two sexes in the language, and different values related to their expression in the form of nouns, pronouns and word genders.

To maintain the neutrality of the sexual dimension of words with the argument: *generic* term for the masculine, *marked* term for the feminine, is unwittingly to admit the inequality of opportunity of the two genders. But the impact of language is so strong that some women want to become assimilated to the masculine generic rather than affirm the value of the feminine as a generic. I think that they are forgetting to consider their status as sexual subjects in both the real and the imaginary, and the economy of the language they speak.

Indeed, if the question of the sex of the subject cannot be erased in the entire world of work and social relations, where a woman is quickly reminded that she is a woman and not a neutral individual, then the same is true in the possession of imaginary property. From this point of view, I feel that the whole debate surrounding the sex of the phallus is more problematic in our languages, in which the object keeps its own gender and does not take that of its possessor. In other words, if in some languages, a woman can claim to have *her* penis, or rather *her* phallus, the same is not true for us. Our languages have a more complex subject ⇆ object structure, one not as directly polarized around possession of the object, since its subject is in a way an effect of it. Our cultures are more elaborate subjectively and it is desirable that they remain so. From this point of view, some Italian Marxists seem to have felt or understood up to a certain point the importance of culture to what is called social justice. Their enquiry or reflection is worth pursuing; it should not be assumed that it is possible to take a theoretical and practical model developed in one language and carelessly import it into another. I am thinking here of the most classic models of Marxism and psychoanalysis. If their contributions are to be truly relevant, they must be appropriate to our Romance languages. Otherwise they may have the very effect that they themselves decry.

Both of these contemporary cultural models have spoken of the irresoluteness of woman. Freud admitted his ultimate incompetence regarding this 'dark continent', and Marx pointed out that the first exploitation of man by man is the exploitation of woman by man, in particular with regard to the division of labour.

How then can this problem of inequality of science and justice in the matter of sexual difference be resolved?

To give women – and men as men, too, incidentally – a subjective chance again, we must re-examine the issue of the rights attributed to each sex, rights understood in the strict legal sense. This does not exlude changes to symbolic systems, but must necessarily accompany them.

4 Elements of a Civil Law for Women

The written law is a law established for a society of men-amongst-themselves. The trend for women to work outside the home and family, their entry into the world of work and public relationships, is raising questions about the current legal system, especially as far as human rights are concerned. The pretext of the neutral individual does not pass the reality test: women get pregnant, not men; women and little girls are raped, boys very rarely; the bodies of women and girls are used for involuntary prostitution and pornography, those of men infinitely less; and so on. And the exceptions to the rule or custom are not valid objections as long as society is for the most part run by men, as long as men are the ones who enact and enforce the laws.

The argument of the plurality of citizens is not valid, either. Society is made up of two sexes, not of 'men': youth, workers, the disabled, immigrants, the unemployed, women, etc. The urgency and simplicity of the legal problem today in terms of human rights causes politicians and jurists to sink into a virtually religious pathos of compassion for sexually neutralized individuals. All other differences are valid except the one that defines a society: sexual difference! There are several reasons for this resistance:

(a) the need to reconsider the separation of church and state

(b) the need to strike a new balance between rights and responsibilities

(c) men's reluctance to admit that women are adult persons that are not reducible to men

(d) men's current incapability of imagining a law to which the concept of equality is foreign.

There are others, including the blind acceleration of our cultures towards an imprecise, even non-existent goal, arising from a reckless concern for profit and an associated unimagined mixture of cultures and languages.

As a woman, I would like to suggest some changes that you – you politically aware women working alongside men – should demand of law-makers in order to establish a civil identity for women. I suggest that rather than fight issue by issue, and always *against*, like little girls or teenagers, you demand rights *for* us women. I admit there will be a negative side to this demand, that is, a part corresponding to women's liberation from subjection under patriarchal law. Unfortunately, then, the first right to be demanded is the right to human dignity.

I shall therefore propose, in a style close to that of the legal code, several points of a legal system adapted to women individuals, starting with this aspect of liberation.

(1) The right to human dignity, thus:

– an end to commercial use of their bodies or images

– legitimate representations of themselves in actions, words and pictures in all public places

– an end to exploitation of a functional part of themselves by civil and religious powers, e.g. motherhood.

(2) The right to a human identity, that is:

– the enshrining in law of *virginity* as a component of female identity that cannot be reduced to money, cannot in any way be converted into cash by the patriarchal family, state, or religion. This component of female identity gives girls a civil status and the right to keep their virginity (for their own relationship to the divine, too) as long as they like, and to bring charges against anyone inside or outside the family who violates it. Although it is true that it is not as common for girls to be exchanged amongst men in our cultures, there are still many places where their virginity is bought and sold, and nothing has replaced the identity status of girls as bodies that men can trade for money. Girls need a positive identity to which they can relate as individual and social civil persons. This autonomous identity for girls is also necessary so that women can consent freely to loving relationships and so that the institution of marriage can be established without alienating women from male power.

– the right to motherhood as a component of female identity. If the body is a legal issue, and it is, the female body must be identified civilly as both virgin and potential mother. This means that it is a woman's civil right to choose to be pregnant, and how many times. She or her legal representative will undertake the civil registration of the child's birth.

(3) Mutual mother–child duties will be defined in the code, so that a mother can protect her children and be assisted by them under the law. This will allow her to bring charges on behalf of civil society when children, especially girls, are raped, battered, or kidnapped. The respective duties of the mother and the father will be covered by another provision of the law.

(4) Women will have the civil right to defend their lives and those of their children, their homes, their traditions and their religion against any unilateral decision based on men's law.

(5) In strictly financial matters:

– Single people will not be penalized by the tax system or in any other way financially.

– If the state wishes to provide family allowances, they will be the same for each child.

– Women pay the same taxes as men for media such as television, so half of all media coverage will be specially aimed at women.

(6) Systems of exchange, languages, for example, will be restructured to ensure that women and men have a right of equivalent exchange.

(7) Women will be represented equally everywhere civil or religious decisions are made, since religion, too, is a civil power.

These are a few examples of priority rights to be written into the law to define women's civil identity. Naturally, this will also entail a redefinition of the rights and responsibilities of male citizens. The delusion of neutral, more or less equal individuals can no longer be perpetuated today, especially after the teachings of Marxism and Freudianism, the women's liberation movements, sexual liberation movements, and social and religious liberation movements, as well as with the blending of cultures we are now seeing, whose esential components deserve serious reflection.

In the world of work in the strictest sense, this neutralization of the sexes is impossible. I shall give three examples that are easy to understand.

(1) For various reasons, women cannot submit to the same rhythms as men, and men's rhythms should not be seen as the norm.

(2) Labour issues, the means and techniques of production, are still for the most part defined by men, and

there is no reason why women should submit to them as if they were the only models or better than those that they would define themselves.

(3) Even in technologies based on language and its coding, it seems a good idea to review women's relations to natural and artificial languages before concluding that their easy access to this type of work represents a social victory for them. It may also contribute to a more subtle alienation of their identity and, thus, to a new type of alienation of society as a whole.

Naturally, the two sexes must have an equivalent right to work and the corresponding wages. But for this social justice to be possible, women must obtain a civil identity simultaneously, if not beforehand; otherwise these rights will never be gained exhaustively, once and for all.

Women must obtain the right to work and to earn wages, as civil persons, not as men with a few inconvenient attributes: menstrual periods, pregnancy, child-rearing, etc. Women must not beg for or usurp a small place in patriarchal society by passing themselves off as half-formed men in their own right. Half the citizens of the world are women. They must gain a civil identity with corresponding rights; human rights, as well as rights respecting work, property, love, culture, etc.

Notes to Chapter 2: How Do We Become Civil Women?

1 Luce Irigaray, *Speculum of the Other Woman*, trans. Gillian C. Gill (Ithaca, NY: Cornell University Press, 1985).

2 By the time this book went to press, the samples were much larger.

3 Luce Irigaray with Rachel Bers *et al.*, *Sexes et genres à travers les langues: éléments de communication sexuée* (Paris: Grasset, 1990).

3

CIVIL RIGHTS AND RESPONSIBILITIES FOR THE TWO SEXES

Florence, 10 September 1988
Unità *Festival*

3

Civil Rights and Reponsibilities for the Two Sexes

I would like to talk to you about women's civil responsibility, to echo a term used by Livia Turco[1] in her presentation for the panel discussion 'Il tempo delle donne' [Women's Time]. This term is dear to me, as it is to her, and whilst I am going to talk about the rights that women must gain, I am also going to talk about their obligations, and their need to enjoy civil rights if they are to respect their own civil rights.

With regard to civil rights and responsibilities, I would like to return once again to the character of Antigone, because of her relevance to our present situation, and also because she is used today to diminish women's role and political responsibility.

According to the most frequent interpretations – mythical, metaphorical and ahistorical interpretations, as well as all those that denote an eternal feminine – Antigone is a young woman who opposes political power, despising governors and governments. Antigone is a sort of young anarchist, on a first-name basis with the Lord, whose divine enthusiasm leads her to anticipate her own death rather than to assume her share of responsibility in the here and now, and thus also in the order of the polis. Antigone wants to destroy civil order for the sake of a rather suicidal familial and religious pathos, which only her innocent, virginal youth can excuse, or perhaps even make attractive.

Today, youth-oriented demagoguery is fashionable; that explains this latest version of Antigone, which I heard discussed on French television this August by men who are supposed to be recognized intellectual and spiritual authorities.[2] This is contemporary culture's interpretation of Antigone, who has become a mysterious figure to us. Antigone is nothing like that. She is young, true. But she is neither an anarchist nor suicidal, nor unconcerned with governing, contrary to what was reasserted on the television programme. It suits a great many people to say that women are not in government because they do not want to govern – but Antigone governs as far as she is permitted to do so. She pits one order against another at the time of the advent of male regal power. Antigone upholds the need to observe order on the following points.

(1) The cosmic order must be observed, particularly sunlight and humanity's earthly home.

(2) Maternal ancestry must be respected, and subjecting it to wars between men over access to power cannot be accepted. Respecting maternal ancestry means taking care of the living bodies borne by the mother, burying them when they are dead, and not preferring the eldest son to a younger (i.e. Eteocles to Polynices), nor a son to a daughter.

(3) These tasks are part of the civil order, with which respect for the gods was linked at that time, for civic

and religious powers were not then dissociated from women's law.

(4) Burial rites are necessary to maintain order in the polis, to protect the earth and the heaven in which it is rooted.

All Antigone's misfortunes stem from the fact that Creon no longer wishes to observe these basic laws. This becomes apparent when the time comes to bury Polynices, when rites must be performed for the dead. Antigone wants neither disorder nor death. She has no a priori contempt for those who govern. She says: 'The law requires burial. It is a civil and religious offence not to bury the bodies of the dead.' She criticizes the king, Creon, for failing to respect order and obey the law; she risks her life doing so, but certainly does not act out of a love of death. Antigone in no way resembles the hot-headed, impatient character with no regard for rights and laws who is proposed to us in a choice between subjective despair or decadent nihilism, with those corrupted by power on one side and suicidal young anarchists on the other. I would like to ask the intellectuals who revel in such dilemmas: 'What do you propose other than the corrupt and the young?' – except your complacent funereal musings, even if they are sincere. Have they not lost interest in life and truth, and is this not, unfortunately, the very reason for their television success?

The true Antigone has nothing to do with these pathetic theatrical exhibitions. Antigone is neither a nervous wreck nor an exhibitionist, and if you want to pay her proper respect, a little more rigour is called for.

Antigone respects the natural and social order by

genuinely (not metaphorically) respecting the earth and the sun, respecting maternal ancestry as a daughter, respecting oral law rather than a written law which is becoming established and which claims to know nothing of the oral. Such is Antigone. Her example is always worth reflecting upon as a historical figure and as an identity or identification for many girls and women living today. For this reflection, we must abstract Antigone from the seductive, reductive discourses and listen to what she has to say about government of the polis, its order and its laws.

In her own way, Antigone indicates a path for returning from the political dimension to objectivity. She asserts that the bombast of seductive, empty discourse, with the aim of obtaining power, sows disorder in the polis, offends the gods, upsets the very cosmic balances themselves.

She reminds us that the earthly order is not a pure social power, that it must be founded upon the economy of the cosmic order, upon respect for the procreation of living beings, on attention to maternal ancestry, to its gods, its rights, its organization.

She says no to men's power struggles, men's conflicts over who will be king, the endless escalation over who will be superior, and at any cost. She attests that the order of the polis and political responsibility cannot imply a conflictual polemic solely in one's own interests, with the aim of gaining 'a place in the sun', or satisfying one's desire, even cupidity, which leads to never-ending wars. She says that the law has a substance and that this substance must be respected.

It seems to me to be worthwhile reconsidering the content of the civil law today, in the light of the truth about Antigone, among other things.

Men have been running society for centuries. They have therefore defined the laws according to their own conceptions – conscious or unconscious, clear or obscure – of the state. They have organized all human groups according to their needs or desires.

The decline of the patriarchal family structure and women's entry or re-entry into the public sphere make new management of civil society a necessity. It is not a question of reviving the civil–uncivil dichotomy between men and women (inside or outside the home), but of reshaping or reorganizing civil society according to current needs.

Today men and women lack civility, and a proliferation of rights regarding the acquisition or possession of property, whether material or even spiritual, will not eliminate the fundamental lack of civility between people. Patriarchy has been organized with an emphasis on wealth rather than respect for life and the intersubjectivity between people necessary for this respect to exist. In our day, we are fascinated by infinite subtleties involved in the manufacturer, commerce and ownership of property. Yet we know practically nothing any more about commerce between people. We are so alienated by goods, money, economic exchanges in the narrow sense, that we are losing our most basic physical and moral health.

I am amazed that most professionals or representatives of spiritual powers talk so much about sex as the site of sin and loss of divinity and so little of money, except perhaps in certain so-called liberation theologies. As if the sin were not the prostitution of sex for money, and respect for sex itself were not the condition of life, love, generation and regeneration of the world.

But since I think that you are already aware of this point, I would like to move on to how to establish or re-establish civil rights and duties for men and women. You will see that the question of respect between the sexes, of an equitable civil identity for each sex, is always bound up with problems of money, or at least with the preference for ownership of property over respect for persons.

Who should we start with, men or women, women or men, in naming areas that lack civility? If I start with men, you will be tempted to say that that is what we were expecting, and to hear what I am about to say as an echo of aggressive accusations rather than to listen to the substance. If I start with women, I will appear to be unfair, at least in my own eyes, for women have no rights as women. How then could they be disrespectful of them? Women's lack of civility derives chiefly from the fact that they do not demand rights that are appropriate to them. I will come back to this. But I would first like to indicate how the current legal system allows men to get away with a chronic lack of civic-mindedness towards women. This keeps women as political wards or treats them as children, which explains why they too often settle for the status of minors or a place on the fringes of society, just as they have developed a loathing of the law because it permits such abuses. This does not resemble the figure of Antigone. Yet in men's abuses of rights, you will see some disorder of the type for which Antigone criticized King Creon, and some elements of female law that should be written into the legal code today.

In her view and mine, it is men who for the sake of money allow themselves to be disrespectful of nature, the sun and the earth, the water and the air, who are uncivil.

It is men who do not care about women's work of procreation, who destroy their own bodies along with those of others for the sake of civil powers or powers of war amongst men, who are uncivil.

Those men, too, who dare to refuse to bury the dead, with the result that they sully the cosmic world, the world of the gods and living beings, are uncivil. And in this case, too, you can understand the legal weight of Antigone's demand of a political tyrant: in her time, Creon.

Men who do not respect women's ancestry, who consider children, and virgin girls in particular, to be their property, are uncivil. Ethnologists theorize that this way of using girls is the basis of culture. The exchange of virgins amongst men is supposedly what defines and maintains the existence of our culture. The only rationalization for such a conception of culture is the taboo on son–mother, father–daughter and brother–sister incest. It is amazing that the lack of actual incest can lead to such possession of girls by their fathers, then their husbands. This is symbolic incest, but real incest also exists, and to a much greater extent that is known. Many of my women friends, many of the women who have confided in me, have been raped one way or another by a male member of their family: father, grandfather, stepfather, brother, etc. If an underage girl seeks help from the state (police, consulate, etc.), she is returned to her rapist, or, in any case, her father. Currently, a girl who is raped by her father or who is a prisoner of the family, in the case of incest within it, has very little legal recourse. While incest and involuntary abortion amongst teenagers who become pregnant as a result do occur, they are not talked about. The state sanctions this barbarity by the heads of families. The mother says nothing because she dares say nothing. She does not know what to say, in any case. She, the mother, has no right with regard to her children against the head of the family, either. At least, for a variety of reasons, her rights are difficult to establish. Faced by these two forms of men's lack of civility,

- possessing virgins to found the symbolic order of their culture, and
- practising real incest within the family,

legal recourse is necessary. I propose that the right to virginity as belonging to the girl, and not to her father, brother, or future husband, should be enshrined in law. In other words, I think that the right to virginity should be part of girls' civil identity as a right to respect for their physical and moral integrity.

Indeed, virginity in the narrow sense involves a physiological problem: the keeping or losing of the hymen. Often men have been interested in only this aspect of things, especially in buying and selling girls amongst themselves. Civil law must also protect girls from all forms of sexual abuse, not just pure and simple loss of virginity; it must guarantee their physical integrity.

Furthermore, from this point of view, men who rape, prostitute, or possess women without their responsible consent, that is, without the subjective reciprocity guaranteed by the law, are also uncivil.

Uncivil, too, are men who abuse the image of women's bodies for pornography and advertising. The law must protect girls' right to moral virginity by imposing images and language consistent with the value of women's sexuality. This means that public signs, as well as mass media programmes and publications, must respect women's sexual identity. It would be a civil offence to depict women's bodies as stakes in pornography or prostitution (passed on by advertising to a greater or lesser extent).

A common excuse, to the effect that this type of sign, by providing an outlet for fantasies, delays or replaces the act, seems to me to be cruelly ironic in so-called civilized societies. This type of statement is clear evidence that, in our societies, women do not have the right to speak, that they are not civil persons in their own right. Women would not argue like this except out of submission to male sexual identity. As long as women have no civil identity of their own, it is to be expected, unfortunately, that they will conform to the only existing models, supposedly neutral, but in fact male. Hence the need to redefine the objective content of civil rights as they apply to men and women – since the neutral individual is nothing but a cultural fiction – and to attempt to establish the legal bases of possible reciprocity between the sexes.

Indeed, men who force women to conform to their standards – not just sexual, but all standards – are uncivil or lack a general sense of civic responsibility. It is therefore unjust that the aims and conditions of work should be defined solely by the world of men-amongst-themselves and that women should be forced to submit to them to earn money legally. Women make up half of human society. It is only just that they themselves should define the standards that suit them but not that they should have to become men in their own right to participate in the public sphere. It is also only just that, as women, they should be able to defend the values they hold dear.

I first cited the defence of their bodies through the right to virginity. Next I shall mention the right to use their bodies freely as far as giving birth is concerned, i.e. the right to choose motherhood. I shall not spend much time on this point because it has often been raised. That does not mean that this women's right should not be written into the civil code definitively and without restriction. In my opinion, it is necessary to give mothers a preferential right with regard to the children that they have borne. Of course, children are conceived by women and men together, but conceived only. The work of gestating, giving birth, breast-feeding and mothering is up to women. Naturally, all over the world, the odd exception can be found where mothering is concerned. But democracy as it is understood forces us to acknowledge that that remains the exception, and I ask myself, and I ask you, why, when women are involved, an exception is always cited as evidence against the norm. Whatever the case with mothering, which men perform as work only exceptionally, women care more about the lives of their children and their physical and moral integrity. It therefore seems necessary that civil society should assist them in this work, that they should be the preferred guardians of their underage children, and that they should have legal recourse against the seduction or rape of their children, against the assault and battery inflicted on them within the secrecy of the family, against the overwork that may be demanded of them. The duties of mothers and children must be reciprocal, in my opinion. A child should therefore have the right and the duty to demand civil help for its mother if she is in danger, as a result of violence or economic hardship, for example. Of course, fathers must keep some rights with regard to their children. But experience shows that their rights must not take priority, because many fathers abuse them or use them without fulfilling the corresponding duties.

This notion of mother–child relationships should, in my view, lead to a change in training for motherhood. This task would become a civil issue, not just a private one, but that is not to say state-run. This would oblige women to respect their children as independent persons, and children to respect their mothers the same way. It would no longer be valid to claim that fathers play an essential role as a third party. Civil society itself would become the third party, and this would confer upon the mother and children responsibility towards it. The father would not be a third party. He is the mother's partner in love, and that is not the same thing. Why should one parent have a two-way relationship with the child and the other parent be the impartial third party? This notion of parental relationships is valid only in a society where men alone are considered to be responsible citizens, and women and children remain minors under male guardianship, or, to put it more bluntly, underdeveloped, ignorant people dependent upon good, solid, real culture decreed by the male masters.

Men's lack of civility begins with this key nodal point: men, and men alone, are capable of running the state, of decreeing its civil and religious standards. According to them, these standards are the truth, and no other is possible. These standards have existed for all eternity, or, at least, throughout what they call History, their History. The rest is only chaos, disorder, darkness, devilry, or obscenity. That is the so-called rational conception of the evolution of humankind. It corresponds to only a few millennia of our culture. Truth and justice demand that we find out how these criteria have been imposed as society's only standards and that those of another culture should be envisaged as possible criteria for civil organization: respect for life, for the one who procreates, for the line of descent that gives birth; respect for nature as fertile, for the dwelling-place, for the goddesses and gods essential to the safety and spiritualization of women and men, for the systems of images and symbols appropriate to the two sexes; respect for girls and younger sons and no exorbitant privileges for the eldest son bearing the family name, and so on.

These standards often amount to an order that does not subject life and its culture to the rule of money. The impoverishment of our world today stems from this inversion: money first, then life, without a rational analysis of the hierarchy of these values. For although money is necessary, it is necessary only as long as it remains at the service of life. Otherwise what good is it?

If men, therefore, in many ways behave uncivilly, and if they seem especially responsible for the inversion of the priorities of life and money, women fail in their duties as citizens in other ways. Men are uncivil as a result of too many rights and too few duties, and women as a result of too few rights and too many duties, for which they compensate by impulsiveness and subjectivity without social bounds, in the form of either persistent childish behaviour or maternal authoritarianism extending into the social sphere.

This is their way of taking part in civil order or disorder, and it was perhaps tolerable as long as it occurred within the secrecy of the family. Women sometimes became nervous wrecks, or they would compensate for their lack of identity through authoritarianism over their children. They also consoled themselves for their servitude through a relative pleasure in being kept, through their desires to receive or buy gifts: furniture, clothes, jewellery, and so on. All this remains an integral part of an economic system in which we still live.

It is becoming increasingly clear that money can never be enough to guarantee either human identity or dignity. The money that women receive as the cost of submission to their husbands and the institution of the family, which is useful to the nation, and the money that they earn themselves and that gives them relative social autonomy and freedom is not enough to confer a civil identity upon them. Women's economic independence makes it all the more obvious that they lack this identity. Women's social visibility is no more useful. It is not enough to make them citizens any more than money is. What can make them citizens are civil rights and duties that are appropriate to them.

The rights women have gained in the last few years are for the most part rights that enable them to slip into men's skin, to take on the so-called male identity. These rights do not solve the problems of their rights and duties as women towards themselves, their children, other women, men and society.

Moreover, the rights gained by women sometimes place them in conflict: they may choose when they want to be mothers, for example, but they do not have a female identity that would enable them to make that choice. Another source of imbalance is that their assimilation of the male identity prevents them from exercising their function of regulating social order; and this provides a good excuse for sending them home under their husbands' guardianship in the hope that women's influence in the private sphere of the family will have a beneficial effect on male public government.

It should be added that the rights gained by women say nothing about women's duties towards one another. A man may do pretty well what he likes to a woman, and the same applies to a woman with respect to another woman. On this point, women's sins are too often left unmentioned or are assessed in terms of passion rather than in civil terms. They are condemned or excused without measure, without objective assessment. The same concessions should be made for them as for children, the oppressed, the ill. It is true that as long as women do not enjoy rights, they will not reach civil adulthood as women. But that is exactly why the demand for rights establishing criteria of their responsibility is justified. Secret relationships, relationships of simple proximity, private guardianship, or spiritual mothering are valuable only as such before or after civil rights are instituted for each woman, and women have obtained the freedom and autonomy guaranteed them by society. It is essential that women should help each other reach private or public adulthood today, and it will always remain desirable, but this assistance cannot take the place of an identity defined in civil terms. Women cannot in some clandestine way confer rights upon one another by renouncing their citizenship. They cannot extend their exclusion from running the state, remain on the fringes of society, substitute themselves somehow or other for the establishment of symbolic organizations valid for all women – those of a country, but also those of the entire world.

Indeed, what is happening with women attests to a need of our societies: they must re-evaluate the right to sexual identity. The sexual dimension (not sexual choice) must be recognized as part of civil identity. This is what will enable us to sublimate sexuality otherwise than through partial drives, the only solution proposed by Freud. According to him and the spiritual authorities that still lay down our law, reproduction is the sole regulator of sexual drives. Yet reproduction has nothing specifically human or sublime about it. The rights to virginity, motherhood by choice, preferential guardianship of children, and caring for the home, means of expression and symbolic relationships are not rights without corresponding duties.

Having rights – human rights in any case – implies having duties. When it comes to property, however, things are not so simple. My purpose in demanding these rights for women is to make them take responsibility for themselves socially, make them responsible adult citizens. It is up to them to protect their virginity, their motherhood, their bit of nature, their house, their images, languages, god(s) or goddess(es). It is therefore up to them to become subjects capable of sublimating their sexual drives, cultivating their sexuality, giving it rhythm, temporality, stakes. To do this women need rights.

All the rights I have mentioned with regard to men's lack of civility would make women responsible for themselves and would not leave them in a position where they are perpetually making demands as social minors. They would become responsible for their own physical and moral integrity, responsible for their child-bearing and their children, responsible for their dwelling-place and their home, responsible for their culture. Women are conscientious. But for them to accomplish a task, the task must be assigned to them. Without such public responsibilities, they remain mired in instability, dissatisfaction, criticism. Only civil rights can emancipate them from these disorderly and often sterile forms of behaviour.

Any social relationship is always to some extent a question of civil rights and duties. How can we, today, restructure the problem of rights for women? Not by leaving them secondary powers, subjective, or rather subjectivist, compensatory powers, a substitute maternal individualism, or licences for pseudo well-being. Women would have the right to be at ease in public places as they have had the right to be at ease in the privacy of homes. We now know what horrors such ease hides. We know to what private or public violence women have been subjected and are subjected, on the pretext of an easier life for them – direct violence or violence mediated to varying degrees by images, symbols, etc. It is not possible for several people to be at ease together except under specific, unusual circumstances. Personally, I have rarely encountered it as the norm in a group setting, even amongst women. Each woman says whatever she pleases, according to her passions, her desire for power, her narcissism, her moods, her limits. Incidentally, these limits are accentuated by two things:

– the lack of adaptation of the symbolic order to women, and

– the profound individual and collective alienation of women that blinds them to themselves and others, especially in public or semi-public behaviour.

In the face of all these difficulties, it is my view that the most imperative needs are definitely:

– to open up all arenas of public expression to women

– to give them work and wages corresponding to their status as adult citizens, and especially

– to give them rights that enable them to escape from the alienation of the family and the state, the world of men-amongst-themselves, but also from the possible alienation stemming from other women.

Giving women individual rights comes down to acknowledging the freedom of each woman and making her responsible for it. The demand for freedom is just. It must be coupled with responsible civil or civic adulthood. The best way to promote this adulthood is to give women the rights appropriate to them and to oblige them to respect these rights, to respect themselves.

This legal step would mean a real historic transformation and not shifts of influences within norms and powers that remain unchanged. The women's liberation movements cannot carry out their mission if they do not demand the institution of civil rights adapted to women: rights regarding their relationships to themselves, their children, men, but also to other women; objective, visible, verifiable rights; rights that are not exercised in secret and in a rather persecutory manner, but that function with a third party as a guarantor – civil society.

The objectivity of women's civil rights should be established on a national level, but should also be covered by international agreements. I do not think that local or national ghettos meet the needs of today's world, even if women's vocation is still to protect dwellings and local sites. One does not preclude the other. By that I mean that a local or national women's law is not suited to the legal needs of all women, which must be redefined in our time. Moreover, local and especially national, power is internationally suspect. A force without a rationale that can be shared beyond the borders of a given country cannot be developed without political risk. Obviously that does not mean that a nation cannot be the first one to make changes in the civil order. It means that reforms regarding sexual identity must potentially be worldwide in scope.

The art of politics, in my opinion, consists in ensuring that the rights and responsibilities of every man and woman are respected, at least within a supposedly democratic system. This political management requires the institution of a new civil code, especially with regard to respect for human rights. Politicians' speeches have become seductive and empty, moralizing and pathetic more often than not (especially as far as workers, the unemployed, youth, the disabled, the Third World, etc., are concerned), except when they degenerate into personal confrontations. It is no longer really a question of civil government. When I listen to politicians' speeches today, I often listen in vain for what regulates the content. I hear varying degrees of skill, varying degrees of intelligence, varying degrees of ignorance. Very rarely do I hear a logical argument spelling out an option for civil organization. The height of the art is to get oneself elected as a democratic candidate without a platform. This perhaps shows a certain degree of familiarity with how transference works. But what does it mean to be elected as a person and not as a platform? I leave it to you to judge. This caricatural case exists. It seems to me the result of reducing eligible candidates to half of the electors. Electing men in itself corresponds to electing a class of persons and not the substance of political platforms. Everything else follows from there. Election speeches are ample evidence of men's desire to hold on to their power in most cases. But why do they want it? That is much less clear. As friends in business said to me during the last French presidential campaign: If they only want to be of service why do they go to so much trouble? Or what is it they're really after?

What is it they are after, indeed? Sometimes I wonder if they have a very good idea of it themselves. In any case, they do not let the electorate in on it. The negative and critical issues are sometimes clear, but the others are non-existent or very fuzzy. 'I want what's good for my country', one of them will say. What does such a statement mean, and what does it say is the objective stake of the democratic decision concerning it? Nothing. It is only a question of allegiance to someone who is supposed to know how to deal with things as they come up. Nowadays, any other thought of a possible future, any project that goes beyond what already exists or the criticism of the past is immediately deemed mystical, or utopian, or demagogic. Especially if it comes from a woman? Is that not how Antigone was just recently described, contrary to reality? She was, in addition, and again contrary to reality – especially historical – compared to the writer Simone Weil. Which does not make much sense except as an effect of a fashion, including a book industry fad, of which Antigone and Simone Weil may both become victims.

We have reached a point of such confusion that the least common-sense statement causes a stir around the world: statements or decisions on disarmament are typical examples. And yet these are only indispensable preliminaries to running a civil society. Civil society, in our time, requires public relationships to be places of reciprocity between individuals. It is not satisfactory that the only civil mediator should be money. It is not satisfactory that relations between persons should be incessantly conflictual and made hierarchical by powers associated with property ownership rather than people's qualities and experience. This undemocratic social structure, which is necessarily individualistic and conflictual, has its origins in the relations between the sexes.

The PCI shows a certain degree of understanding of this issue, which, incidentally, is dealt with by Marxist theory. I hope that it carries out or supports through legislation this consciousness-raising about the ongoing exploitation of one sex by the other, an exploitation that determines most if not all other types of social alienation. This process would draw on qualities traditionally associated with the PCI – particularly a desire not to separate the economic from the cultural – making it possible to propose programmes for intelligent and peaceably practicable social transformation.

Notes to Chapter 3: Civil Rights and Responsibilities for the Two Sexes

1 See note, page xviii.
2 Programme called *Océaniques* on *Antigone*, August 1988, with Pierre-André Boutang and George Steiner.

4

THE FORGOTTEN MYSTERY OF FEMALE ANCESTRY

Syracuse, 31 March 1989
The municipality and Ombre publishing house

Palermo, 3 April 1989
D. Women's Research Centre and University (Social Psychology)

Terni, 2 June 1989
The municipality, Project Woman

4

The Forgotten Mystery of Female Ancestry

In some ancient yet very advanced traditions, it is the woman who initiates the man into love. This initiation does not mean making use of a whole set of tricks to awaken some basic sexual pleasure [*jouissance*] in the man; neither is it the same as female seduction in accordance with the most rudimentary of male instincts. These patterns of behaviour are the mere relics of woman's role in love. Today's pornography trade would have us believe that eroticism boils down to that, that we humans are capable of nothing else. Eroticism is supposedly a drug for us, a means of forgetting ourselves, the prostitution of women to male drives, the 'little death' for men, a fall, annihilation, etc.

Freud theorized that this form of love was the only one possible. And the most intelligent men – and occasionally women – of our time have maintained that eros is chaos, darkness, bestiality, sin, annihilation, but that we must submit to eros to relieve our tensions, unburden ourselves of them, 'shoot off' and rest again.

Poor Eros! Poor love! All the more so since contemporary culture can no longer even imagine that it might be mistaken or might change on this score. This is eros, and what is not eros is agape: love without eros. If you do not want to fall or sin, you abstain from sex. If you agree to fall, you can disguise the fall or atone for it by using it to procreate.

What has become of us, that we are so poor in love? But our poverty does not preclude all kinds of pornographic and theological complexities. We have become unisex in our drives. That means that we have returned to the chaos that preceded human differentiation, and that there eroticism is a sort of blind, virtually incessant drive incapable of establishing its own rhythm or harmony, of taking or giving shape, except through reproduction. We have returned to primitive chaos, which according to our mythology is neutral-male. The only thing that enables us to emerge from this undifferentiated abyss is our own manifestation in the children we beget. Our attractions, our loves, our embraces, are supposed to have become chaotic once more, short of individuation, undefined in terms of our human appearance. We are supposedly neither man nor woman because we are not yet men and women; we are still in the abyss of the undifferentiated human being, the male pole of the most primeval Eros.

Does Freud not describe the libido in precisely this way? Male, or at best neutral, and therefore akin to the primitive chaos preceding the definition of persons, and, particularly, definition in terms of their sexual affinity.

In that historical and/or mythical time, a time that is still with us, Eros urges coupling only for the purpose of producing descendants and causing more clearly manifested forms to appear. Eros urges neutral Chaos and the Earth, Gaia, to couple, so that they produce offspring in whom they discover their own forms.

The first offspring of the male abyss were Erebus and Night, then Ether and Day, first as space, then as time. On Gaia's side, the first to be brought forth were Uranus (Heaven) and Pontus (Sea), which delimited and defined her as Earth, as the female pole, and in relation to which or to whom she gave birth.

By compelling entities that were still fairly undifferentiated sexually – Chaos and Gaia – to couple, Eros made them give birth to sexual beings. Sexual difference thus made its appearance through the children conceived. But the male pole of the first couplings prevented his children from being born because they would have kept him from being the only lover on earth. He tried to force them to remain in their mother's womb, causing her to suffer terribly. Her youngest son therefore castrated the insatiable lover and murderous father, doing so from within his mother's very body, when Uranus drew near. The blood from the castration fell upon the earth, and of it were born the Erinyes (Furies), the Giants and the nymphs called the Meliae. The son cast the genitals into the sea, the sperm floated to the surface, and Aphrodite was born of this foam. She was conceived in rather the way fish are: outside the mother's womb and without copulation.

According to Hesiod, Aphrodite was conceived in the sea by the sperm of Uranus, or, in other versions, especially the one recounted in the Homeric hymns, by Zeus and Dione. Here the role of Dione, a little-known deity, is to give birth to Aphrodite by Zeus. She is the female equivalent of Zeus: Dione means Goddess [*Dieue*].[1]

According to an older, more cosmogonic tradition,

then, Aphrodite is the daughter of the sea, fertilized by the divine sperm of Uranus (Heaven) without personal coupling. She is the daughter of more male and more female cosmic poles born of Gaia, conceived and carried in the liquid element of the universe, outside any human body.

Contrary to what people say, myths are neither univocal nor timeless. And Aphrodite, like all the great divinities of antiquity, is represented in a variety of ways. A version that is later than the one in Hesiod's cosmogony (which does not necessarily signify that it was written later, even though its meaning is later in the order of appearance of the beings of this world) explains Aphrodite's birth as that of a daughter begotten by God and Goddess, thus a daughter of the Gods of the male and female gods. In this case she would be a unique phenomenon in our cultures.

Aphrodite thus holds a very special place between nature, gods and human manifestation. She represents the embodiment of love, already sexualized in its forms – man and woman – but still close to the cosmos. This human love emerges in a woman. Contrary to what is popularly said or believed, Aphrodite is not a figure or deity who incites sexual debauchery, but one who manifests the possible spiritualization of blind drives or instincts through tenderness and affection (see Hesiod, *Theogony*, 205–6, for example). These qualities of love are not inconsistent with the carnal act; on the contrary, they give it its human dimension. In Greek, Aphrodite's specific attribute is called *philotes*: tenderness. It therefore is not a matter of agape without eros, but of the two combined in a love that is both carnal and spiritual.

This definition of love requires a clear distinction

between the sexes, a distance between them, and between them and the cosmos, so that they are not reduced either to constant copulation or to coupling for the sole purpose of procreation.

Aphrodite – in her time – was the embodiment of love becoming human freedom and desire. This embodiment is female and represents almost the exact opposite of Eve the seductress. She is the spirit made flesh, especially in relations between the sexes, thanks to the goddess's female *philotes*.

This assumes, of course, that the woman is free to act and speak, and that she uses her freedom to deify our human bodies, and not to make them revert to the animal or undifferentiated elemental state. The elevation of love to its human and divine identity is, from the point of view of the genesis of our culture, woman's concern. And when women are banished from love or dispossessed of it, when their divinity as lovers is forgotten, love once more becomes drives that verge on animality, disembodied sublimation (?) of them, or death.

Destroying or forgetting *philotes* in love reestablishes a sort of primitive chaos, in which the male instinct is the relatively neutral agent, or a place beyond human embodiment, a reversal or overturning of primitive chaos into a single male God who no longer teaches us the divinity of love between woman and man.

This sending back, displacement, or ecstasy of chaos into the Beyond, without proper sublimation of love between human beings, leaves us without laws regarding the difference between the sexes and respect for nature as micro- and macrocosm. Procreation thus becomes necessary as a way out of chaos and as a means of suspending perpetual coitus.

From this perspective, it is understandable that love should appear to be a sin. Indeed, it destroys human identity. It annihilates bodies and spirits in a drive towards perpetual, undifferentiated coupling, without rest or respite, without intelligence or beauty, without respect for living human beings, without proper deification of them. In this unceasing drive, the very rhythms of natural growth – and particularly those of birth – are abolished, as this drive is akin to an imperialistic neutral-male that has been uprooted from the space-time of life on earth.

We are not far removed today from this primitive chaos. Freud's theories both show it at work and sustain it. According to Freud, the libido is actually closely related to the male or neutral drives corresponding to what the stories of the myths (History in the form of myth?) describe as the manifestation of the sexuality of the primitive male pole: Uranus.

Of course, it might be possible to sublimate partial drives: we could transform our exhibitionistic or voyeuristic desires through play-acting, for example. But nothing could enable us to sublimate genital drives, those corresponding to sexual difference *per se*. Procreation is supposedly the subsistence, transformed into religious and civic duty, of a way of coping with the ever-present primitive chaos.

This chaos could be called life drives, in that it is an attraction with no relation to the individuation of persons; it is a male or neutral attraction determined no doubt by a desire to return to the mother's womb and enjoy exclusive possession of the fertility of the womb in order to maintaine one's own vitality. The most positive aspect of love would still be the desire to return to the procreating whole, regardless of the body or sex of the procreator. The most negative aspect would be the need to destroy, even oneself, even life and the life-giver, by destructuring any cohesiveness. This would amount to reducing every entity to its tiniest atoms with no possibility of its becoming whole again.

Of course the negative side of death drives is fairly apparent. What has been emphasized very little, even blindly contested, is the destruction at work in life drives themselves, in so far as they do not respect the other, and in particular the other of sexual difference. If Freud ended his life so pessimistic about the future of culture, and if psychoanalysis has had highly problematic effects on private and public relationships, it is fundamentally because Freud talked only about primal male sexuality, and because limiting oneself to just one of the poles of sexual difference amounts to limiting oneself to the chaos of a primitive desire that preceded any human incarnation. Freud's man resembles the Uranus of Greek mythology, who has no other desire but to commit incest continually, and who wants no children to result from this coupling – not out of virtue, but out of jealousy, because his children would limit his infinite power and boundless attraction. In this scheme of things, the abyss therefore does not correspond to the female sex, but to the lack of rhythm and harmony of male desires, which specifically refuse any manifestation of the difference between the sexes so that they can appropriate the fertility of the mother's body.

Urged by eros, man immerses himself in chaos because he refuses to make love *with* an other, to be *two* making love, to experience sexual attraction with tenderness and respect. Male sexuality has once again annihilated human individuation, notably by entrusting the man, not the woman, with the responsibility for eros: this would mean entrusting this responsibility to both, in accordance with tradition. The most common type of Western sexuality, the one described by Freud, the one forbidden or censured by spiritual authorities but promoted through advertising and the media without any concern whatsoever for people and unrestricted by consistent civil regulations, is an elemental male sexuality, supposedly irresistible and useful for the reproduction of the species – a sexuality that has destroyed the *philotes* of Aphrodite.

Today it is accepted that it is the man who must initiate the woman into love, and that he may do it with neither education nor experience, as if, by virtue of being a man, he is knowledgeable in love. Most often, the man does not initiate the woman into anything much, except perhaps a pleasure that society does its utmost to forbid her to enjoy except with the man, in order to induce her to worship him. This pleasure revealed by the male lover is the outcome of instincts and male drives whose residual human aspects are often singularly difficult to define (unless it is perhaps the man's obscure need to return to the mother's womb, if this much can be said to be human). The man/lover thus induces the woman to forget herself, to fall from herself, although the fall may procure her pleasure. By this I mean that (with rare exceptions) there is no longer anything very subtle or spiritual about the initiation into love, and that this initiation does not take into consideration the different qualities of men and women so as to embody them fully. It is accepted that eros destroys identity, not that it fulfils it. Which always amounts to reverting to an economy of desire preceding Aphrodite's birth, to the desire separate from love that psychoanalysts talk about, for example.

The path to reciprocal love between individuals has been lost, especially with respect to eroticism. And instead of contributing to individuation, or to the creation or re-creation of human forms, eroticism contributes to the destruction or loss of identity through fusion, and to a return to a level of tension that is always identical, always the lowest, with neither development nor growth. Eros could only return to a sort of zero point, a sort of state of equilibrium for man – and so is not likely to have a positive future here on earth.

This notion of love has led women to forget themselves, to submit childishly or slavishly to male sexuality, and to console themselves, through motherhood, for their fall and exile from themselves. Motherhood – promoted by spiritual leaders as the only worthwhile destiny for women – most often means perpetuating a patriarchal line of descent by bearing children for one's husband, the state, male cultural powers, thereby helping men escape from an immediate incestuous desire. To women, more secretly, motherhood represents the only remedy for the abandonment or for the fall inflicted in love by male instincts, as well as a way for them to renew their ties to their mothers and other women.

How have we come to this – all of us, and especially we women? One of the lost crossroads of our becoming women lies in the blurring and erasure of our relationships to our mothers and in our obligation to submit to the laws of the world of men-amongst-themselves.

The destruction of female ancestry, especially its divine aspect, is recounted in a variety of ways in the Greek myths and tragedies. Aphrodite's mother is no longer mentioned; she is supplanted by Hera, and Zeus remains the God who has many lovers, but no female equivalent. The goddess Aphrodite can thus be said to have lost her mother. Iphigeneia is separated from her mother to be offered as a sacrifice in the Trojan War. And though oracular speech was originally passed on from mother to daughter, beginning with Apollo it is often assimilated to the oracle at Delphi, which still has a place for Pythia, but not for mother–daughter relationships. Antigone's uncle, the tyrant Creon, punishes by death her faith, her loyalty to her maternal ancestry and its laws, in order to safeguard his power in the polis. The Old Testament does not tell us of a single happy mother–daughter couple, and Eve comes into the world motherless. Although Mary's mother, Anne, is known, the New Testatment never mentions them together, not even at the moment of the conception of Jesus. Mary goes to greet Elizabeth, not Anne, unless Elizabeth is Anne, as in Leonardo da Vinci's interpretation. Mary's leaving her mother for a marriage with the Lord is more in keeping with the tradition that was already several centuries old.

Perhaps the best illustration of the fate of the mother–daughter relationship is to be found in the myths and rites surrounding Demeter and Kōrē. You are probably fairly familiar with these myths. You live in a place that still bears traces of them, memories of them. As is almost always the case, there are several versions of the myths. This means that they appeared at different times and in different places.

Most ancient Greek myths are of Asian or unknown origin. This is true of those concerning Aphrodite, Demeter and Kōrē/Persephone. Their evolution should be understood as the result of migrations to different places where they were adapted to varying degrees, and the effect of historical developments. For myth is not a story independent of History, but rather expresses History in colourful accounts that illustrate the major trends of an era. The temporality of History is expressed in this form because in those days, speech and art were not separate. As a result, they retained a special relationship to space, time and the manifestation of the forms of incarnation. History as expressed in myth is more closely related to female, matrilineal traditions.

In myths concerning mother–daughter relationships and myths about the goddess/lover and god couples, the story, setting and interpretation were masked, disguised to varying degrees by the patriarchal culture that was growing up. This culture erased – perhaps out of ignorance, perhaps unwittingly – the traces of an earlier or contemporaneous culture. Thus many sculptures were destroyed or buried in the ground, rites were eliminated from traditions or transformed into patriarchal rituals, myths and mysteries were interpreted from the patriarchal perspective, or simply as representing the Prehistory of the patriarchal era.

The same applies to the myths of Demeter Kōrē/Persephone. It seems to me that there are at least two different versions. In one, Demeter's daughter is abducted by the god of shadows, fog and the Underworld, and then seduced by him despite herself, so that she cannot return to her mother for good. When she is first carried off by Hades – also called Erebus or Aidoneus by Homer – she is looking at spring flowers with other maidens, and just as she is about to pick a narcissus, the earth opens up, and the prince of the Underworld takes her away with him. He has not yet made her his wife when Hermes, Zeus' messenger, comes to fetch her at the request of Demeter, her mother, who in her grief has made the earth barren. The god of the Underworld has no choice but to obey, but he gives Persephone a poisoned gift behind Hermes' back: he gives her pomegranate seeds to eat, and anyone who accepts a gift from Hades becomes his captive.

This is the version of the Homeric hymn. In later versions or interpretations, Kōrē/Persephone has become more or less responsible for her own fate, and is thus more like Eve the seductress, who leads man to his fall. It was nothing like that in the initial versions. But the story of Demeter and Kōrē/Persephone is so terrible and so exemplary that it is understandable that the patriarchal era wished to make the seductive woman bear the responsibility for its crimes.

It seems that Kōrē/Persephone's only sin was to reach out to pluck a narcissus. Of course it is preferable to leave flowers rooted in the earth rather than pick them, especially in spring, but should the girl be punished for picking a flower, even a marvellous narcissus, by being carried off to the Underworld?

Whatever the reasons cited for blaming Kōrē/Persephone, it is clear that her fate is decided by men-gods. Jupiter [Zeus], Poseidon and Hades must divide up the heavens, the sea and the Underworld. The episode of Kōrē/Persephone's abduction involves a power struggle between Zeus and Hades, two brothers of different parentage who can neither meet nor see each other because of their ancestral ties. Zeus is a descendant of Gaia, and Hades is a descendant of Chaos. Zeus is a child of the female pole, conceived with one of her first sons; Hades, or Erebus, is the offspring of the initial Chaos, or the male pole of the origin of the world. Zeus wishes to become God of gods despite the infernal male powers that wanted to annihilate him as an individual more differentiated than Chaos. He wants to overturn the divine male omnipotence of the initial Chaos.

To do this, Jupiter, Kōrē/Persephone's father, gives his daughter in marriage to Hades, who none the less steals and rapes her. This episode, like many others, takes place at the time of the shift from matrilineality to patrilineality. Jupiter trades his daughter's virginity for affirmation of his male omnipotence. His father did not want him to be born as a human manifestation having a sex; he agrees to yield his daughter's virginity, her female identity, as the price of his recognition as God of the Olympian gods. To exist as God in the eyes of all, he agrees to give his daughter in marriage to the god of the Underworld. This transaction takes place without the consent of either his daughter or her mother. Two things are thus sacrificed to establish Zeus' power: Kōrē/Persephone's virginity and the love between Demeter and her daughter. Jupiter has no right to use his daughter and her mother this way. Demeter tries to tell him so, but Kōrē/Persephone no longer dares, except by crying for help. Jupiter breaks off the exchange of words between his daughter and himself at the same time as he deprives her of her virginity, a good bartered with Hades.

This sacrifice of Kōrē/Persephone's virginity and language, including that used in her relationship with her mother, seems to show that Jupiter does not yet have access to either fulfilled humanity or the divinity of his male identity. Yet not only does he make Hades bear this imperfection, but he continues to commit incest and to have many lovers, which indicates that he is not fully embodied.

By affirming himself as sovereign of the world above, he creates or maintains the existence of a sovereign of the world below. If he reduplicates heaven, Jupiter must also reduplicate the earth. According to the patriarchal hierarchy, both human and divine, Jupiter is above Uranus in access to the celestial, but this above implies a below. The infernal Hades corresponds to the sovereign Zeus. The two of them can neither see nor meet each other. The God of the world above is the resplendent, dazzling, yet thundering God of lightning, of the violent relationship between heaven and earth. The god of the world below is the god of indifferentiation transformed into the Underworld, fog, abyss. This infernal power of the realm of the male gods, this god of the invisible, is a thief, a rapist, the black man all little girls fear. Is he not Jupiter's dark double? Is he not the shadow of sovereignty? Is he not the inverse [*envers*] or inferno [*enfer*] of his absolute power without tender sharing with the other sex? Does this Hades not correspond to the dark underside, or, in current parlance, the disordered unconscious of his brilliance?

So the black man takes her, little girl or adolescent. He cloaks her in shadow. He carries her off to his underground domain. She refuses to give herself to her lover.

She cries out when he drags her down to the Underworld, but neither her mother nor her father, Zeus, hears her. It is said that the sun hears her, and perhaps Hecate does, unless it is the sun that tells Hecate of Kōrē/Persephone's abduction.

It is Hecate who, ten days later, tells Demeter where her daughter is. She also tells her that the abduction took place with the connivance of Zeus, husband of the one and father of the other. Demeter then becomes angry with the gods. She leaves Olympus and goes among the mortals. Grief-stricken, she tries to console herself by becoming the wet-nurse to another child. Without revealing her identity, she offers her services at a house where a woman has just given birth to an unhoped-for younger son, a late son, perhaps a son of a god, of Zeus. Her offer is accepted.

She is given a little boy to care for in place of her daughter, and for a while she is content. But she has plans for this child. She wants to make him immortal. She therefore brings him up in a strange manner: she does not feed him, but rubs him with ambrosia, blows on him while clasping him to her heart, and at night holds him in the fire. That is how someone is made immortal. Indeed, the child grows up like a god. But his mother watches Demeter tending her son. She becomes frightened and cries out, giving away her presence. Demeter, vexed at the mortal woman's lack of confidence in her, drops the infant, leaves him on the ground, and decides to stop working for the household. She then reveals who she is and demands that the husband make amends for the offence.

The essence of her demand is that a sanctuary to her should be erected at Eleusis, and this is done. Demeter retires there and thinks of nothing but her daughter. Her grief causes the earth to become barren, which means no more food for the mortals, and therefore no mortals to honour the gods.

After a year of famine, Zeus becomes worried. He tries to persuade Demeter to change her mind. First he sends Iris, then all the gods in existence, as messengers of peace, bearing magnificent gifts and all the privileges she could want. But Demeter accepts nothing. She wants to see her daughter's face again. In this regard, it should be noted that she never turns to her mother in her grief. Like Kōrē/Persephone, like Iphigeneia, like Antigone, like Mary and like Eve; none of these women has a mother in whom to confide. The female line of descent is already interrupted.

The story of Kōrē/Persephone shows that the daughter is not responsible. The mother is a little more responsible, for she begins to console herself for the disappearance of her daughter by nursing a boy-child. But her acceptance of this substitute is also a form of revenge. A god has stolen her daughter, so she renounces life among the immortals and tries to force a mortal upon them as a god. When this solution fails, she refuses any proposition from the God of gods, unless he gives her back her daughter. Zeus understands that there is no other way to save the mortals and the immortals. He sends Hermes to Erebus [Hades] to fetch Persephone. Hades must obey, but he is still plotting to keep his mastery: he induces Persephone to eat a pomegranate seed, which, unknown to her, makes her a hostage of the Underworld.

Mother and daughter are happily reunited. Demeter asks Persephone to tell her everything that has happened to her. She does so, beginning at the end. In a way, she goes back in time, as must any woman today who is trying to find the traces of her estrangement from her mother. That is what the psychoanalytical process should do: find the thread of her entry into the Underworld, and, if possible, of her way out.

But let us return to the reunion of Demeter and Persephone. They spend all day pouring their hearts out to each other, comforting each other, expressing their joy to each other. Hecate joins them and, ever since, she has held an important place in the mysteries surrounding Kōrē/Persephone. In particular, she follows her when she descends to the Underworld and precedes her on her return to earth.

Indeed, the poisoned gift that Persephone accepted from Hades is apparently enough to make her his captive at least a third of the year, the cold season. Similarly, yet differently, eating an apple is all it later took to be excluded from earthly paradise. Then, it is true, the prohibition was clearly stated before the sin was committed, which was not the case for Kōrē/Persephone. But both are stories of fairly similar traps or taboos involving flowers or fruits; in one, the prince of darkness is clearly responsible, and in the other, a woman is blamed. It is true that Eve is no longer a woman, since she is made from Adam's rib. Eve is only part of Adam, created without a mother; this is not the case of Kōrē/Persephone, who is a goddess, a daughter of a goddess, of a god couple. The bond between humanity and divinity is thus unbroken. Sometimes it is woven in one direction, sometimes in the other, with curious tests or tricks, strange prohibitions imposed upon women to establish a patriarchally transmitted ancestry and theology.

All these codes are beyond the little girl. She may make a mistake, but she does not decide to do so. She is caught up in the dealings, contractual or otherwise, between men, between men and male gods. According to their agreements, she should refuse everything from men and gods so that she will not be seduced through a mistake on her part. She should keep well away from mankind, men's contracts, men's relationships, until her virginity is no longer a subject of negotiations between men. She should remember that virginity signifies her relationship to her physical and moral integrity, and not the price of a deal between men. She should learn to keep herself for herself, for her gods and her love, for the love of which she is capable if she is not taken outside herself, abducted, raped and deprived of freedom of action, speech, thought. Obviously this freedom must be real and not controlled; the freedom to seduce in accordance with male instincts or to gain equality of rights within a unisex male order is only a superficial freedom that has already exiled woman from herself, already deprived her of any specific identity. She thus becomes a sort of puppet, or movable object, reduced to being subjected to basic drives with passive goals. She thinks she needs to be 'screwed' by a man, she suffers from a basic oral need (partially an inverted projection stemming from male desire), Freud writes learnedly, without considering that this need might be symptomatic of woman's submission to male instincts. According to Freud, this need is a sort of relic of the initial chaos that male desire opened up in the earth's womb.

Indeed, this chaos still exists. It is manifested in the libido's economy of drives without genitality, the economy in which woman is imprisoned. One of the two – he – is stuck in incestuous regression and anal possession, while the other – she – is reduced to oral mendicancy. Woman supposedly always hungers for him without any return to herself. She thus eventually becomes hungry from the abyss that he has opened up in her; she becomes ill with a bottomless hunger, because it is not her hunger, but the abyss inside her of the natural and cultural hunger of the other.

None of this could happen if she had not been separated from her mother, from the earth, from her gods and her order. This is the original sin that makes woman a seductress against a backdrop of nothingness. But why abduct her from her mother? Why destroy female ancestries? To establish an order man needed, but which is not yet an order of respect for and fertility of sexual difference.

To make an ethics of sexual difference possible once again, the bond of female ancestries must be renewed. Many people think or believe that we know nothing about mother–daughter relationships. That is Freud's position. He asserts that on this point, we must look beyond Greek civilization to examine another erased civilization. Historically, this is true, but this truth does not prevent Freud from theorizing on and imposing, in psychoanalytical practice, the need for the daughter to turn away from the mother, the need for hatred between them, without sublimation of female identity being an issue, so that the daughter can enter into the realm of desire and law of the father. This is unacceptable. Here

Freud is acting like a prince of darkness with respect to all women, leading them into the shadows and separating them from their mothers and from themselves in order to found a culture of men-amongst-themselves: law, religion, language, truth and wisdom. In order to become a woman, the virgin girl must submit to a culture, particularly a culture of love, that to her represents Hades. She must forget her childhood, her mother; she must forget herself as she was in her relationship to Aphrodite's *philotes*.

If the rationale of History is ultimately to remind us of everything that has happened and to take it into account, we must make the interpretation of the forgetting of female ancestries part of History and re-establish its economy.

The justifications given for breaking up mother–daughter love are that this relationship is too conducive to fusion. Psychoanalysis teaches us that it is essential to substitute the father for the mother to allow a distance to grow between daughter and mother. Nothing could be further from the truth. The mother–son relationship is what causes fusion, for the son does not know how to situate himself in regard to the person who bore him with no possible reciprocity. He cannot conceive within himself. He can only artificially identify with the person who conceived him. To separate himself from his mother, man must therefore invent all sorts of objects for himself, even transcendental ones – gods, Truth – in order to resolve this insoluble relationship between the person who carried him inside her and himself.

The situation is different for the daughter, who is potentially a mother and can live with her mother without destroying either one of them even prior to the mediation of specific objects. To them, nature is a preferred environment; the ever-fertile earth is their place, and mother and daughter coexist happily there. They, like nature, are fertile and nurturing, but this does not prevent them from having a human relationship between them. This relationship depends upon the establishment of female lines of descent, but not solely. Therefore the daughter's words to the mother may represent the most highly evolved and most ethical models of language, in the sense that they respect the intersubjective relationship between the two women, express reality, make correct use of linguistic codes and are qualitatively rich. For little girls, education, the social world of men-amongst-themselves and the patriarchal culture function as Hades did for Kōrē/Persephone. The justifications offered to explain this state of affairs are inaccurate. The traces of the story of the relationship between Demeter and Kōrē/Persephone tell us more. The little girl is taken away from her mother as part of a contract between men-gods. The abduction of the daughter of the great Goddess serves to establish the power of male gods and the structure of patriarchal society. But this abduction is a rape, a marriage with the consent of neither the daughter nor the mother, an appropriation of the daughter's virginity by the god of the Underworld, a ban on speech imposed on the girl/daughter and the woman/wife, a descent for her (them) into the invisible, oblivion, loss of identity and spiritual barrenness.

Patriarchy is founded upon the theft and violation of the daughter's virginity and the use of her virginity for commerce between men, including religious commerce.

Carrying on this commerce involves money changing hands, but also exchanging real property; at stake are either symbolic or narcissistic powers. Patriarchy has constructed its heaven and hell upon this original sin. It has imposed silence upon the daughter. It has dissociated her body from her speech, and her pleasure from her language. It has dragged her down into the world of male drives, a world where she has become invisible and blind to herself, her mother, other women and even men, who perhaps want her that way. Patriarchy has thus destroyed the most precious site of love and its fertility: the relationship between mother and daughter, the mystery of which is guarded by the virgin daughter. This relationship does not separate love from desire, or heaven from earth, and it knows nothing of hell. Hell appears to be a result of a culture that has annihilated happiness on earth by sending love, including divine love, into a time and place beyond our relationships here and now.

To re-establish elementary social justice, to save the earth from total subjugation to male values (which often give priority to violence, power, money), we must restore this missing pillar of our culture: the mother–daughter relationship and respect for female speech and virginity. This will require changes to symbolic codes, especially language, law and religion.

Notes to Chapter 4: The Forgotten Mystery of Female Ancestry

1 *Dieue*: Irigaray has put the feminine *e* ending on the masculine *dieu*, and has also capitalized it. The usual term for goddess is *déesse*–Tr.

Lecture Dates

'A Chance to Live', Tirrenia, 22 July 1986
'How Do We Become Civil Women?', Rome, 8 April 1988
'Civil Rights and Responsibilities for the Two Sexes', Florence, 10 September 1988
'The Forgotten Mystery of Female Ancestry', Syracuse, Palermo, Terni, 31 March, 3 April and 2 June 1989

Index